W9-BGL-517

WITHDRAWN

Summary

Volume I
Second Edition

Edited by Wornie L. Reed

William Monroe Trotter Institute
University of Massachusetts at Boston

1990

Table of Contents

Preface

In the Spring of 1987 the William Monroe Trotter Institute at the University of Massachusetts at Boston initiated a project entitled, "The Assessment of the Status of African-Americans." Thirty-five scholars were organized into study groups, one for each of six topics: education; employment, income, and occupations; political participation and the administration of justice; social and cultural change; health status and medical care; and the family. The study groups were established to analyze the status of African-Americans in each of the topical areas in anticipation of the results and analyses of the National Research Council's Study Committee on the Status of Black Americans. We wanted to have the widest possible discussion of the present condition of blacks and the social policy implications of that condition.

The multidisciplinary group of scholars comprising the study groups included persons from all sections of the country and from varied settings–private and public universities, historically black universities, and private agencies. A list of these scholars by study group is given in the Appendix. Each of the study groups met and drafted an agenda for examining significant issues under their respective topics. Members chose issues from this agenda within their areas of expertise and identified other scholars who had written extensively on other issues on the agenda. These other scholars made a variety of contributions, including original papers, reprints, notes and materials, and/or substantial commentaries on draft documents.

Despite the pressures of limited time and limited financial support for this work, six volumes were produced:

Volume I: *Summary*
Volume II: *Research on the African-American Family: A Holistic Perspective*
Volume III: *Education of African-Americans*
Volume IV: *Social, Political, and Economic Issues in Black America*
Volume V: *Health and Medical Care of African-Americans*
Volume VI: *Critiques of the NRC Study,* A Common Destiny: Blacks and American Society

Each of the study groups developed its own conclusion and policy recommendations.

In addition to study group members and other contributors, we are indebted to a number of individuals for the production of this study. We owe thanks to Phillip Hallen and the Maurice Falk Foundation for underwriting the costs of producing these volumes. Special thanks are also offered to the following persons: our editors–Duncan Nelson, Manuscript Editor; Linda Kluz and Suzanne Baker, Production Editors; the office staff–Eva Hendricks, Gemima Remy and Tina Wilson; and Assistant Director Frances Stubbs.

Wornie L. Reed

1

Stratification and Subordination: Change and Continuity

E. Yvonne Moss and Wornie L. Reed

One of the measures used to gauge progress made by African-Americans in gaining equal opportunity has been to compare and contrast the status of black Americans to that of white Americans using various social indices. Historically, the status of blacks relative to whites has been one of subordination; race has been a primary factor in determining social stratification and political status. Relations between white and black Americans were established during slavery and the Jim Crow era of segregation. In the infamous *Dred Scott* (1856) decision, U.S. Supreme Court Chief Justice Taney articulated the fundamental nature of this system of racial stratification: "Blacks have no rights which whites are bound to respect" (Bell, 1980a).

James Baldwin perceptively observed that in the sea change from the old worlds to the new, French, English, Spanish, and other Europeans "became white," while the Tokolor, Mandinka, Fulani, and other Africans "became black" (Baldwin, 1985). Black and white became racial labels denoting power and status. Blacks were slaves; whites were free. Elimination of property requirements in the nineteenth century extended the franchise to all white men and the passage of the Nineteenth Amendment (in the twentieth century) extended the franchise to white women. Not until the passage of the Voting Rights Act of 1965 was the franchise extended to all black Americans; and not until the *Brown* decision of 1954 were black Americans granted equal protection under the law. The Civil War outlawed slavery, but it did not eliminate stratification and privilege based on race. White domination continued through segregation laws and practices. The *Brown* decision, the civil rights movement, the Civil Rights Act of 1964, and the Voting Rights Act of 1965 ushered in a new era of race relations. After 300 years of slavery and 100 years of legalized racial oppression, the relations between white and black Americans were now to be based on "equality." The "age of equality," however, has not been accompanied by an end to white domination.

Scholars in this study have sought to evaluate developments in race relations, particularly since 1940, by examining racial stratification, subordination, and change in various areas of American life. Our general conclusion is that despite improvements in various aspects of American life, racial stratification has not changed in any fundamental sense. In addition to the structural mechanisms that perpetuate differential status researchers point to social factors–attitudes, values, ideology, and racial violence–that reinforce racial domination. Legal doctrines and the courts have always provided justification and legality for whatever structural form the system of racial stratification has taken. Historically, the U.S. Constitution has been one of the primary supports for white supremacy.

From Slavery to Equality

Relations between black and white Americans are now established by the equality expectations based on the Constitution. This document, which originally sanctioned slavery, then segregation, has since 1954 given legal sanction to the principle of equality. At the time of the American Revolution slavery was sanctioned by the Constitution as a form of white property rights. The concepts of equality articulated by colonists in revolt blurred class distinctions between poor and rich whites, promoting affinity and solidarity at a time when these class distinctions could have undermined the war of liberation against the British.

After independence, an expansion of civil liberties for whites was accompanied by a contraction of civil rights for blacks. Slavery, recognized in the Constitution as a political and economic phenomenon rather than a moral one, provided the essential ingredient by which lower-class whites and upper-class whites could share a common identity as "free men." Slavery, and the racism that justified it, provided a way by which poor whites could simultaneously feel superior to enslaved blacks and equal to rich whites in spite of a distinctly different social and class status. In order to maintain this white American kinship, there was the need to keep black Americans in "their place." Citizenship, national identity, and social status in the emerging United States were increasingly defined in terms of race and color. Although Jacksonian Democracy removed property qualifications to extend the franchise for white males, in 1840 most free blacks were legally denied the right to vote.

From the beginning, the Constitution gave the wealthy "planter class" (approximately 7% of all slaveholders) disproportionate power, both nationally and locally. A majority of the justices on the Supreme Court between 1789 and 1865 were themselves slaveowners. Up until the Civil War, constitutional interpretation did not violate the economic and political imperatives of a slave economy dominated by a white, male, landed aristocracy.

After the war, the Civil War Amendments (Thirteenth, Fourteenth, and Fifteenth) along with Reconstruction, provided a halting start toward a new basis of race relations. These nascent efforts were brought to an end, however, with the Hayes-Tilden Compromise in 1877 and the withdrawal of Union troops from the South. Racial discrimination against blacks increased at the same time that political democratization increased for whites. In a major test of the Fourteenth Amendment, the Supreme Court legitimized corporations but not the rights of black citizens in the 1873 *Slaughterhouse Case(s)*. In those cases, the due process clause of the Fourteenth Amendment, which would become so vital to the restructuring of black/white relations in the mid-twentieth century, was interpreted to provide more protection for corporations (deemed legally to be "persons") than to African-Americans (Bell, 1980b).

The struggles of black Americans and their allies against segregation during the nineteenth and twentieth centuries culminated in the *Brown* decisions (1954 and 1955), the Civil Rights Act of 1964, and the Voting Rights Act of 1965. The White House's support for the modern civil rights movement of the sixties seemed to herald at long last the arrival of the equality revolution. For the first time since the existence of the Freedmen's Bureau during the Reconstruction period, governments not only made laws but constituted themselves as instruments of egalitarian policy. Above all, the courts were now obliged to examine constitutional principles in the light of egalitarian pressures.

With the emergence of the "age of equality," a number of important questions have been raised about race relations, law, and stratification. Can equality expectations eliminate racism and stratification by race and assure that there are no special advantages distributed according to race? Are there economic incentives and penalties capable of inducing the white elite to forsake segregation? And, is it possible that equality will actually sustain, rather than relieve, white domination?

Examination of the issues raised by such questions has led some scholars to argue that although the application of equality is perceived as the extension of democratic principles to all–regardless of race, creed, color, or sex–it is more likely that the equality principle is serving white interests more than those of black people. Historically, advances for African-Americans have been the result of policies primarily intended to serve white interests rather than to provide remedies for racial injustices (Bell, 1980b). Thus, scholars need to examine the contemporary "age of equality" for mechanisms that promote white self-interests at the expense of African-Americans.

For instance, one social analyst concludes that just as segregation "shifted" racism out of slavery to assure white exploitation of black labor, so equality "shifts" racism out of segregation to assure the economic demise rather than the exploitation of black people. Socioeconomic disparities coexist with the opportunity for equal rights under the Constitution. Supreme Court rulings have not outlawed racism, it is argued, but instead have actually endorsed a new form of racism to justify white oppression of black Americans. The notion of equality today, then, is as much a racist doctrine as were slavery and segregation before (Wilhelm, 1987).

The established image of "equality" has meant that African-Americans can possess all manner of civil rights in the abstract, but little property. Wealth remains in white hands so that even under this so-called "equality" the social results are the same. The equality doctrine both masks and justifies the prevailing inequalities. Mechanisms other than color distinction are employed to subjugate black citizens. Growing disparities between black and white Americans coincide with the legal expansion of equal rights. The vigorous replacement of segregation by equality occurs at the same time that black people are being eliminated from the economy.

Socioeconomic Status

Economically, black America is in crisis. The annual income of black families is 57% of white families. The net worth of black American families in 1986 was $3,397, compared to $39,135 for whites families, a difference of almost 1200%. In 1985 a National Urban League study indicated that with persistent unemployment and expanding poverty, African-Americans were being left out of the nation's economic recovery. If current trends continue to the year 2000, only 30% of all black men will be employed. Just as the abolition of slavery did not eradicate racism nor the patterns of structural bias based on race, the equality doctrine has also failed to do so. Ironically, contemporary interpretations of the equality principle based on the Constitution seek a "color-blind" society that perpetuates inequality based on race.

When economics, employment, and social class are examined the continued importance of race is clearly evident. While discrimination has lessened in jobs and training programs, racially exclusive practices remain. Limitations on mobility because of race affect the black elite as well as the black poor. The most strikingly favorable indication of racial change is the growth of the middle class among African-Americans. In 1982, using constant dollars, almost 25% of black families had incomes over $25,000 as compared to 8.7% in 1960 (Taylor, 1984).

This occupational mobility is a product of three factors: affirmative action, the expansion of public sector employment, and higher levels of education. Between 1966 and 1982 the number of black college students increased from 340,000 to over one million. A number of indicators, however, tend to suggest that such mobility may be slowed if not reversed in the near future. Between 1980 and 1984, black college enrollment dropped by 3%. Concomitantly, the more precarious economic status of black members of the middle class makes them more vulnerable than their white counterparts to economic downturns, government budget cuts, and changes in affirmative action policy.

The black middle class is proportionately smaller than the white middle class and is skewed more toward the lower than the upper part of the statistical group. Black professionals occupy lower paying jobs in lower prestige fields than white professionals. Black families tend to be more dependent on two or more wage-earners to maintain their middle-class status than are white families. Higher proportions of married women in black households work than married women in white households. These factors along with a lower net worth and fewer resources means that black middle-class families are not as able as white middle-class families to transmit their class position to their children. In some cities–Atlanta, Philadelphia, New York, Los Angeles, Chicago, Oakland, and the District of Columbia, for example–the growth of middle-class economic status is still significant. However, there is less hope generally for economic advancement for other African-Americans trapped in poverty in urban and rural areas than there was in the sixties.

Noteworthy progress was made between 1959 and 1969 in reducing poverty among African-Americans. The percentage of black citizens who were poor dropped in that decade from 45% to 25%, and the official black family poverty rate declined from 48% to 28%. The net reduction in the number of poor black families was 494,000. However, during the 1970s this black economic progress was reversed as the percentage of blacks who were poor in 1979 had declined less than one-half of one percent during that decade, from 28% to 27.6%, and the black portion of the poor increased to 31%. Over 300,000 more black families were poor in 1979 than in 1969, thus canceling the gains made in the previous decade (Cross, 1984).

The dimensions of the socioeconomic crisis are even more evident from an examination of the consequences of these worsening economic conditions. More than one-half of all black children grow up in poverty. Unemployment among black teenagers has increased. Many young black men, unsuccessful in school and unable to find legitimate work, turn to hustling and crime. Homicide has become a leading cause of death among young black females as well as among young black males. The economic crisis among the poor has reduced the proportion of black men who work. Traditionally, blacks have been more likely than white men to be in the labor force. Since 1970, however, blacks have been less likely to be in the labor force (Swinton, 1990) and many of these workers are unemployed or underemployed. Some analysts estimate that less than one-half of black men are engaged in steady work.

In the area of housing, racial bias has remained pervasive. Throughout most of the half century that the federal government has been involved in housing and urban development, national policies have compounded and supported the discriminatory practices of realtors, banks, insurance companies, and lending companies. A review of major national policy initiatives by officials in the legislative, executive, and judicial branches of government indicates that during most of the past 50 years federal policies favored segregation and discrimination in housing.

Before 1962, there were three separate housing markets: black, white, and mixed. This situation was supported by federal housing policy in the interest of promoting "homogeneity in neighborhoods." A presidential executive order (11063) issued in 1962 did little to foster fair housing practices. Similarly, the Civil Rights Act of 1964, so important in other areas, had little impact on open housing. The Civil Rights Act of 1968 was the first attempt to develop a comprehensive fair housing program. Discrimination was made illegal, with some exemptions, in almost all housing. But the law provided more symbolism than substance. Because it was not enforced it had little impact even during national administrations that were favorable to the concept. During the Reagan administration, predictably, even less was accomplished. Discrimination in housing remains widespread, as several studies have demonstrated.

Not only have government policies failed to appreciably diminish racial discrimination in housing, but, unhappily, urban development programs and progrowth coalitions have pursued urban renewal projects that have destroyed housing, dislocated the poor, and reduced the housing stock in the cities. In addition, there has been little discussion and consideration given to the goal of increasing home-ownership among black Americans.

Residential segregation of black citizens is increasing throughout the nation. Taeuber and Taeuber's national housing segregation index indicates that America's cities are only slightly less segregated today than they were in 1940. The index in 1940 was 85.2. By 1950 that figure had worsened to 87.3. In 1960 there was a slight drop to 86.1, but the segregation index increased during that decade to 87.0. The decade from 1970 to 1980 showed a drop from 87.0 to 81.0. Clearly, America's neighborhoods continue to be "homogeneous" (racially segregated) despite new laws and public proclamations (Reed, 1989).

Discriminatory practices were reinforced by the patterns of suburbanization after World War II. This suburbanization was supported by government loans and financial policies. But the suburbs were for white households, not black: between 1950 and 1970 African-Americans accounted for only slightly more than 5% of suburban residents. Most black residents who live in suburbs today live in those that are directly adjacent to the nation's largest cities. Fair housing practices have been virtually nonexistent in America's suburbs.

The slow desegregation of white suburbs and neighborhoods is only one aspect of the housing crisis. Progress toward access to safe, affordable, adequate housing has been nil. Public housing projects have generally been failures; often these projects have further isolated poor black people from the rest of society. Inadequate delivery of public services and the absence of competitive and diverse private retail and financial services contribute to the general crisis in housing as well as to other aspects of social and economic deprivation.

White Attitudes

Economic and social deprivation have been the consequences of racial stratification. The system of domination that institutionalizes race-based access to opportunity structures is both reflected in and reinforced by attitudes of white and black Americans. It is interesting to note that the longest running topic in survey research has been the evaluation of white attitudes towards African-Americans. Since World War II, issues related to race in survey research have changed in two ways: the kinds of issues addressed and the ascriptive characteristics associated with the attributes "progressive" and "regressive." Changes in law have made many issues moot. Surveys of white attitudes today indicate that regional differences are less distinct. White attitudes toward black Americans have become more uniform throughout the country.

White Americans still exhibit the duality of orientation that Ellison (1964) labeled "ethical schizophrenia" in the 1940s. By this he meant that white Americans demonstrated a sincere belief in the values of democracy, while condoning and justifying decidedly undemocratic treatment of black citizens. Today scholars use the term "symbolic racism" to explain how white Americans can hold egalitarian general racial attitudes at the same time as they disapprove or oppose policies that seek to operationalize equality. Thus, in general terms, white Americans adhere to principles of racial equality and interaction; but in specific contexts of interaction with black Americans, actual practice does not allow the principle. One explanation for this paradox lies in the degree of intensity of white contact with black Americans. As long as the intensity of interracial experience is low, whites indicate a willingness to participate in that experience. When the intensity increases, tolerance for interaction wanes. The racial attitudes of whites are directly proportional to the amount of interaction structured by the potential interracial context.

Not much change in racial attitudes is expected among white citizens in the near future because whites do not indicate a willingness to choose interracial contact. Contemporary surveys of whites indicate a reluctance to live with black neighbors, a desire to insulate themselves from contact with black people, and a desire to maintain a social distance from black Americans even while agreeing to formal legal and civil rights for black citizens. This suggests an insularity at the core of Euro-Americans racial attitudes that may persist for some time. Such conclusions imply an even greater imperative for legal interpretation and government enforcement to promote equal justice and to move towards the breaking up of systems of white domination.

Value Orientations of Blacks

Stratification by race in America has also influenced the development of values among African-Americans. Here, care should be taken–heeding the admonitions of Ellison–not to equate all value orientations among black people as reactions to white domination. The complex relations between the dominant white American culture and the black American subculture creates a variety of sources for the development of social values among African-Americans. Scholars categorize these sources under two typologies: the traditional American value heritage, and ideological orientations within black communities. While more work needs to be done on regional variations, rural orientations, and relationships between the two major types, four categories of value orientations have been identified within urban black communities: (1) socially integrated, (2) structurally integrated, (3) structurally isolated, and (4) the excluded sector.

Black people who evidence socially integrated values generally maintain contact with black churches, social clubs, and voluntary associations, even though these are primarily oriented toward the values of the white communities where they live. They wish to be "Americans" in the general sense, although the degree to which this means that they wish to be assimilated as "white" Americans is not clear. Individuals of this orientation are success-oriented, and they demonstrate little support or empathy for confrontational racial protests. Members of these black families develop racially self-directed and self-maintaining values at the same time as they develop civil rights and public-policy values for use in the larger, white, bureaucratic, formal world. Black families in this category who live and work in desegregated areas tend to equip themselves to live in two different social worlds.

Members of the structurally integrated category work and sometimes live in integrated settings. Most, however, live–and all of them socialize–in a segregated world. Those who live in black neighborhoods do so because they want it that way. They evidence a split value system. On the one hand they live and work by general "white" American values. At the same time, they articulate well-known black values: that "black is beautiful"; that black history is an important part of their heritage; that black English is acceptable; and that black people are as intelligent and capable as white people. Additionally, they exhibit vigorous civil rights and public-policy values.

Black people in the structurally isolated category are generally employed in low-skilled and service sectors of the economy. The class system in the United States isolates these citizens. The economic and work values of those who are structurally isolated are developed through jobs where workers tend to feel cheated and oppressed by those in control. Therefore, the orientation of these black people is not toward traditional values but toward communal and ideological values of black communities, although some of the traditional values of the group coincide with those of the dominant American values (i.e., values of Southern black culture and black church culture). Blacks in this category tend to advocate the self-regarding and self-maintenance values of popular black culture. They acknowledge the importance of black history, culture, and society. Black English is legitimized and black heroes and heroines are idolized. These values sustain the sense of self-worth, boost morales, and serve to legitimize the cause of black people in the white-dominated society. Other value orientations among this group emphasize liberation, creative expression, and achievement. They support civil rights legislation and enforcement as well as the expansion of those gains already made. Collective action and confrontation are viewed as legitimate ways to pursue the struggle for black rights.

Members of the excluded sector are at the bottom of society in terms of economic and social indices. They are marginally employed or unemployed. They have little education and few marketable skills. Black people in this category are ill-housed, excluded from participation in the larger community, and alienated from the general society. Communications are generally broken with family, church, schools, media, and service agencies. Street life, the primary source of the development of values, does not function well to communicate and transmit traditional American values. In any case, many traditional values and social rules are ineffective in the real worlds that these people inhabit. Families in this grouping who stay in tune with traditional values are the exceptions.

Where do values come from in this grouping? They are improvised, borrowed, and developed pragmatically. Traditional values come to be viewed in pejorative and threatening terms. Indigenous values and norms are legitimized and enforced. There is evidence of hostility towards those in white communities as well as suspicion and distrust of white authority, especially the police. Members of this category exhibit support for civil rights efforts.

Elijah Anderson's work on marginally employed or unemployed black men in Chicago suggests a slightly different interpretation. According to Anderson, there are special hangouts in the cities that serve as gathering places for the urban poor and working-class people who seek a sense of self-worth and status through their sociability and interaction with peers. Urban taverns and bars, barbershops, carryouts, and their adjacent street corners and alleys are examples of the places that serve similar functions for the poor as more formal social clubs or domestic circles do for the middle and upper classes (Anderson, 1978).

Those who frequent these places create their own local, informal, social stratification system. Status within this system is action-oriented and precarious, based in large measure upon what people think and say and do about other members of the group. Extended primary groups develop in these places. Among the groups studied by Anderson the primary values were a "visible means of support" and "decency" (1978, p. 209). Residual values or values group members adopt after the "props" supporting decency have been judged to be unattainable or unavailable are "toughness," "gettin' big money," "gettin' some wine," and "having some fun."

> Some writers have attempted to explain "low-class" values as weak imitations or approximations of the wider society's values. Rodman (1963), for example, has suggested that low-income people are unable to meet the larger society's standards of social conduct and therefore must stretch their own values to adjust to their particular life circumstances. Although there may be a certain amount of truth to this view, and it is supported by my own analysis, I believe it does not go far enough in appreciating the lives of the people involved and the internal coherence and integrity of their local stratification systems. The people I studied... appear not so much to "stretch" a given set of values to meet some general standard as to *create their own particular standards of social conduct* [emphasis added] along variant lines open to them. (Anderson, 1978, p. 210)

While this brief attempt to categorize black value orientations does not cover the entire spectrum of attitudes and values to be found among African-Americans, what is clear is that racial domination and the subordinate position of black Americans in society do influence the values espoused by black people as well as white people. The duality of values held are reminiscent of the concept of "twoness" employed by W. E. B. Du Bois in his 1903 book, *The Souls of Black Folk*. Interestingly, the reality of black peoples' lives, even for those who are classified as socially integrated, is one in which individuals and families exist in two different worlds, two different cultures, between which they must negotiate their existence.

Scientific Racism

There are in the dominant culture a number of mechanisms that reinforce and support white domination. These include ideologies of white supremacy. The most blatant contemporary ideological rationale for white domination is scientific racism. Scientific racism is rooted in the idea that domination is a right of the biologically superior. Scientific racism has produced "evidence" sustaining the belief that black people are inherently inferior, thus, rationalizing white rule.

The proponents of scientific racism advance arguments like those advocated by Social Darwinists earlier in this century. They argue for an educational system that will train the intellectually inferior for specific positions in the labor force. Also, again like the Social Darwinists, advocates of scientific racism view intelligence and achievement as products of innate genetic or cultural endowment. The logic of this has significant and potentially dangerous implications for social policy. If intelligence, achievement, mobility, and success are the products of inherent biological or cultural differences that cannot be altered by environment, then it is folly to try to alter social structures or institutional practices to promote equality or equal opportunity. Scientific racism goes further than Social Darwinism in not only blaming the victim but also in providing a quantitative and quasi-scientific basis for perpetuating inequality and domination.

Traits presumed to be biologically determined become the basis for social policy. This substantially limits the opportunities for targeted groups and makes them the victims of exclusion, sometimes even of extermination. In this century, Nazi Germany is associated with the most developed and horrifying application of social policy based on ideas of scientific racism. Here in the United States, prominent writers and scholars have contributed to the development of this phenomena, especially during the 1920s and 1930s. From the turn of the century through the 1930s scientific racism gained popularity in the United States in scholarly and popular literature. The enactment of the 1924 restrictive immigration bill may have been the highwater mark of the influence of these ideas during that period.

From the 1930s until the 1960s scientific racism was dormant. Now, however, the arguments have been resurrected in new forms. Gone are the archaic notions of phrenology and craniology that assumed that human worth and behavior could be determined by body type. Contemporary theorists seek instead to prove the primacy of heredity over environment in the determination of intelligence. The language is new, but the message is the same: genetic endowment is the great divider between superior and inferior types. Such differences cannot be mediated through legislation or social policy. Hence, racial differences are an immutable fact that are ordained genetically.

Scientific racism has functioned as an influence on public action. Such perceptions of human differences are a convenient *raison d'etre* for a stratified society. Some of the earliest theorists of the ideology of scientific racism were social scientists (Hofstadter, 1959; Schwendinger and Schwendinger, 1974). Preoccupied with social order and progress, they framed questions of individual and social difference as political questions. Their ideas, like all pseudo-scientific ideas regarding the human species, found acceptance among those seeking to justify the subordination of others. In periods of major social change such ideas tend to intensify as status positions are challenged. The 1960s was such a period.

The *Brown* decision (1954) altered the legal status of African-Americans and proved to be a catalyst for the modern civil rights movement. The court's ruling also struck at the core of the ideology of scientific racism. The philosophy of separate but equal had existed under the assumption of biological differences. Thus the ideology of scientific racism had given support to those who sought to maintain entitlement and privilege.

Scientific racism sees entitlement as a just reward to those who are genetically superior. Conversely, genetic inferiority is seen as the basis for restricting entitlement and privilege. Because of the presumptions about the association between race and superiority and inferiority, race becomes the key variable in restricting or granting entitlement. Members of the white race, designated by the ideology as biologically superior, are thus entitled to a superordinate status and the social, economic, and political privileges that are accorded this status. Members of the black race, designated by the ideology as biologically inferior, are denied any entitlement and privileges and are relegated to a subordinate status.

The *Brown* decision was a critical turning point not only in education but in the larger society because it set the stage for major alterations in the system of entitlement. The court's decision not only called into question the denial of choice in education, but also suggested a tolerance for a realignment in the historic patterns of power. The sociopolitical movements of the 1950s and 1960s vigorously sought such a realignment in the patterns of power relations, challenging the entitlements and privileges historically bestowed on white Americans.

The reemergence of the ideology of scientific racism during the past two decades has taken the form of an attack on the mental capacity of black children—and, by implication, all black people—by means of a dubious and abusive interpretation of intelligence testing. Arthur Jensen at the University of California at Berkeley, William Shockley of Stanford, and Richard Herrnstein of Harvard were in the forefront of a debate over the education of black children, the use of intervention strategies, and the development of public policy options to limit population growth among "genetically inferior blacks." All of these concepts were based on presumptions that intelligence was 80% inherited and 20% environment. Thus, policies that tried to use public funds or initiatives to improve the education and performance of black children were deemed to be undemocratic because they granted the disadvantaged some unearned privilege.

The proponents of scientific racism ignored evidence of historical, social, and structural influences on intelligence testing and ignored the decline in SAT scores among white students as well. The emphasis on quantitative data, performed in an advocacy manner, was an attempt to give the resurfaced ideology of white supremacy an aura of scientific objectivity and respectability. The appeal to the inheritability of intelligence restates the same argument that social classes are products of differential genetic stock. Scientific racism is an attempt to make inferiority a matter of science rather than prejudice.

W.E.B. Du Bois identified science and empire as the preeminent values in Western societies at the turn of the century (Du Bois, 1968). It should come as little surprise, then, that science during this century has been enlisted to justify political domination. The ideology of scientific racism has been invoked, in its least harmful form, as a rationalization for the insulation of privilege, the restraint of mobility, and the limitation of entitlement. In its most virulent form, scientific racism is a prescription for genocide.

The history of scientific racism is indicative of how data that purports to be "objective" may be used to promote reprehensible policy. Scientific racism has justified the deaths of countless millions of people by validating the claim that they were inferior and undeserving. A version of this ideology is being used today to justify the continuation of white domination and privilege.

Racial Violence

In a racially stratified society, racial violence is used as a method of social control to maintain the structures of subordination. In a conspicuously violent society so stratified, violence is used for political purposes to maintain a racially bifurcated system, controlled politically by whites.

Historically, patterns of racial violence in the United States have moved in cycles of latent and aggressive activity. Latent periods have been relatively benign. During these periods the superordinate-subordinate system of race relations has been characterized by a kind of white paternalism. Aggressive periods have ensued when the system of domination has been challenged and/or the benefits of white superordination have been perceived to be eroding. During these periods, aggression and violence have been used to terrorize black people; the foundations of racial progress built by blacks have become targets for attack. The ebb and flow of racial violence has followed shifts in the national political economy and changing patterns in the labor force and the labor markets.

All institutions in American society have been permeated by the stratified and segmented nature of race relations. Racially motivated violence is a legacy of these unequal race relations, and it is endemic to the national political culture. Although manifest throughout American history, racial violence has differed in form and significance, breadth, and intensity from period to period.

This racially segmented social structure, established and maintained by violence, generates both systematic oppression of nonwhite racial groups, especially African-Americans, and systematic privileges for whites. The system of white privilege provides the philosophical and material basis for racism among whites. These privileges are the "white rights" that those who perpetuate racial violence are dedicated to defending.

Economically, black people were subjugated in such a way as to ensure their economic exploitation. African-Americans had no significant influence or control over economic production and commerce; indeed, their lives and their labor were "owned" by slaveowners and later by industrialists.

The flipside of this system of racial oppression is the system of social, economic, and political privilege for white Americans. White supremacy and racial oppression have been major factors in the political and economic development of this nation. The function of racial violence has been to establish and to perpetuate this system of differential privilege and deprivation based on race. Racial violence is a deliberate activity that reinforces ideologies of racial supremacy and intimidates the victims of violence and racial oppression.

Racial violence is currently on the upturn, a reaction to two important social dynamics: (1) the dramatic changes brought about by progress in civil rights; and (2) the dramatic transformations in the infrastructure of national economic life which since the Great Depression have generated unprecedented levels of unemployment, poverty, homelessness, and social dislocation. Currently, large segments of the American population are experiencing a heightened sense of insecurity and vulnerability.

During the past decade several research centers have collected information on racially-motivated violence.[1] A study of the data reveals an upsurge of racism and racist violence, with the most deadly attacks coming against the African-American community. There has been an increase in the number of incidents of white mobs attacking blacks in segregated residential areas. There has also been a steady increase in the fire-bombing of homes purchased by black families in predominately white neighborhoods. A study of violence in residential neighborhoods conducted by the Southern Poverty Law Center indicates that between 1985 and 1986 there were at least 45 cases of vigilante activity directed at black families who were moving into predominantly white communities. In the last five years incidents of racial harassment or violence have been reported on over 300 college campuses (Wilkerson, 1990).

The events in Howard Beach that led to the death of Michael Griffith in 1986 and the killing of Yusef Hawkins in Bensonhurst in 1989 reflect a long-standing problem of racist violence in white communities in New York City. Racially motivated assaults had increased to at least one a week in 1987. The Chicago Police Department reported a 58% increase in racial attacks for the first six months of 1986 over the same period in 1985. The New York City Police Department reported an increase in racially-motivated violence over the last eight years. These attacks go mostly unreported in the news media.

The Community Relations Service of the Justice Department and the Center for Democratic Renewal provide data that demonstrate a sharp upturn nationally in violent racial attacks. The increase was 42% between 1985 and 1986, fueled largely by the boldness of white terrorist groups in the United States. Nationally, the Community Relations Services of the Justice Department reports an increase in all cases of racial confrontations from 953 in 1977 to 1,996 in 1982. The Justice Department also reported a 460% increase in cases of racial violence involving the Ku Klux Klan between 1978 and 1979 , and a startling 550% increase in the period 1978 to 1980.

Racial Change Since the 1960s

As a result of the Civil Rights Act of 1964 and the Voting Rights Act of 1965, the decade of the 1960s was a time of significant change in race relations in the United States. Consequently, it is a good reference point from which to begin an examination of trends and developments in the status of African-Americans. However, because racial change has been uneven, it is not possible to concisely summarize its direction over the past two decades.

The greatest changes have taken place in the political sphere. Black mayors are leading—or have led—all of the largest cities in the United States; and they preside over many medium-size cities as well. Although this has often entailed administering central cities burdened with well-nigh unsolvable problems within the context of a dominant white power structure, the new black political influence has also, on the plus side, democratized access to municipal and public service jobs.

The rise in black elected officials has been spectacular: the number increased from 280 in 1965 to 6,681 by 1987 (Boamah-Wiafe, 1990). Yet the fact that that figure represents less than 1.5% of all political officeholders shows that the degree of underrepresentation remains as significant as the gains (Joint Center for Political Studies, 1985).

Discrimination in jobs and training programs has definitely lessened over the past two decades. Yet racially exclusive practices still exist. Many small-sized firms (the fastest growing segment of the economy) exclude blacks and other minorities. And while affirmative action regulations constrain larger companies from such direct discrimination, ways are still found to insure predominantly white work forces—for example, by avoiding areas of large black populations in the location of plants.

These economic developments have had adverse effects on the integrity and unity of the black community. The nuclear family has been weakened by joblessness and by the single-parent trend. The extended family is no longer strong enough to fill the gap as successfully as it did in the past. Drugs and crime also divide the community, creating a climate of fear and distrust. Even in street life there is less solidarity than in the past. The increasing distance between the classes makes it harder for the community to act with a unified voice. And integration, with all its positive features, has also weakened the traditional institutions of the black community: black businesses, black colleges, and even the black church.

Some observers have lamented what they call the "loss of African-American community." Some of this loss can be attributed to the economic bifurcation of the community and the resulting loss of community infrastructure. In addition, there has been a significant loss of black principals, vice-principals, guidance counselors, teachers, and coaches, as a result of school desegregation. Usually, desegregation has meant that blacks have moved into white-dominated institutions, and the schools they left have been reassigned to other purposes or closed. Seldom has it meant that whites integrated into institutions that have been traditionally black and where blacks hold some of the power and influence.

Conclusion

Significant changes have occurred in the racial landscape of America during the past 30 years. However, the basic structural position of African-Americans is the same. Prospects for improving this situation may be significantly affected by impressions held by white Americans about the status of black Americans. Most whites believe that blacks are approaching parity in areas like housing, health care, employment, education, and treatment by the criminal justice system—a perception markedly different from that of most blacks.

In a NAACP Legal Defense Fund study (1989), more than two-thirds of blacks, as compared with one-third of whites, felt that blacks had fewer employment opportunities than whites of similar income and education. In answer to the question of whether blacks received equal pay for equal work, whites responded yes more than twice as often as blacks. Two-thirds of blacks felt that blacks had poorer housing and less access to housing, while only 41% of whites felt that way; twice as many whites as blacks thought that blacks were treated as well as whites by the criminal justice system. As the NAACP Legal Defense Fund study concluded, these gaps in perception—and between perception and reality—need to be addressed by the nation's leaders. These opposing views regarding the parity of blacks and whites in society present a significant impediment to racial progress.

Notes

1.   Including the Southern Poverty Law Center, The Center for Democrats Renewal, the Klan Watch Network, the Joint Center for Political Studies, and the Newsletter on Racially Motivated Violence.

References

Anderson, E. (1978). *A Place on the Corner.* Chicago: University of Chicago Press.

Baldwin, J. (1985). Lecture. First Baptist Church of America, Providence, RI.

Bell, D.A. (1980a). *Civil Rights: Leading Cases.* Boston: Little Brown.

Bell, D.A. (1980b). *Race, Racism, and American Law* (2nd ed.). Boston: Little Brown.

Boamah-Wiafe, D. (1990). *The Black Experience in Contemporary America*. Omaha: Wisdom Publications.

Brown v. Board of Education, Topeka, Kansas 347 U.S. 483 (1954); 98 L. Ed. 873; 745. Ct. 686.

Cross, T.L. (1984). *The Black Power Imperative* (Rev. ed.). New York: Faulkner Books.

Du Bois, W.E.B. (1961). *The Souls of Black Folk*. Greenwich, CT: Fawcett. (Originally published 1703.)

Du Bois, W.E.B. (1968). *Dusk of Dawn: An Essay Toward an Autobiography of Race Concept*. New York: Schocker Books. (Originally published 1940).

Ellison, R. (1964). *Shadow and Act*. New York: Vintage.

Hofstadter, R. (1959). *Social Darwinism in American Thought* (Rev. ed.). New York: G. Braziller.

Joint Center for Political Studies. (1985). *Black Elected Officials: A National Roster*. Washington, DC: Joint Center for Political Studies.

NAACP Legal Defense Fund. (1989). *The Unfinished Agenda on Race in America*. New York: NAACP Legal Defense and Education Fund.

National Urban League. (1985). *The State of Black America*. New York: National Urban League.

Reed, W.L. (1989). *African Americans and Social Policy in the 1990s*. Occasional Paper No. 17. Boston, MA: University of Massachusetts at Boston, William Monroe Trotter Institute.

Rodman, H. (1963). The Lower Class Value Stretch. *Social Forces, 42* (2), 205-215.

Schwendinger, H. & Schwendinger, J. (1974). *The Sociologists of the Chair*. New York: Basic Books.

Swinton, D.H. (1990). Racial Parity Under Laissez-Faire: An Impossible Dream. In W.A. Van Horne and T.V. Tonnesen (Eds.), *Race: Twentieth Century Dilemnas–Twenty-First Century Prognoses*. Madison, WI: University of Wisconsin, Institute on Race and Ethnicity.

Taylor, W.L. (1984). Access to Economic Opportunity. In L.W. Dunbar (Ed.), *Minority Report*. New York: Pantheon.

Wilhelm, S. (1987). Paper prepared for the Assessment of the Status of African-Americans Project. Boston, MA: University of Massachusetts at Boston, William Monroe Trotter Institute.

Wilkerson, I. (1990, May 9). Racial Harassment Altering Blacks' Choices on Campus. *New York Times*, pp. 1, B10.

2

Race and Inequality in
the Managerial Age

William Darity, Jr.

In the evolution of American social relations an important transformation has taken place from capitalism to the managerial estate, from the dominance of the captains of industry and finance to the dominance of the intellectuals and the intelligentsia. The change is manifest in the authority given to experts in social analysis, policy making, and management. Within this transition, race and ethnicity continue to exercise decisive roles in dictating patterns of individual achievement and opportunity in the United States.

In particular, discrimination in its most encompassing sense continues to be operative, although laws have been passed to make certain of such practices illegal. These laws have been circumvented, ignored, or gradually rolled back; in many instances the laws have not touched critical sites of discriminatory activity. To the extent that American society is intensely hierarchical, there is an incentive for members of ascriptively differentiated groups to coalesce and carve out occupational and status niches. Antidiscrimination laws certainly were not designed to level the hierarchical structure of U.S. society; hence the driving motive for discrimination as exclusion remains strong.

Alterations in the structure of the U.S. economy–associated with the social transformation from capitalism to managerialism–have meant that those with low skill levels have been barred, because of the increased competition as positions diminish, from older occupations to which they once had access. Concomitantly, this same form of discrimination means that large numbers of blacks also are denied access to the newer occupations.

These are the circumstances that accompany justified concerns over the perpetuation of an American "underclass," disproportionately black, reproduced from generation to generation. This underclass is a consequence of social forces that are being unleashed as capitalism gives way to the managerial estate. These forces play out along the dimensions of class, race, and ethnicity, and they structure patterns of inequality in American society. And in addition to the persistent interracial gap between blacks and whites, there is also an intraracial gap that demands assessment. In a society with an increasingly bifurcated employment structure, where occupational growth is concentrated in low-wage, low-skilled jobs and in high-wage, professional positions, the mass of blacks–to the extent that they find employment at all–are concentrated in the former set of jobs. This concentration aggravates the degree of polarization between the majority of blacks and the relatively small percentage of blacks who hold professional level positions.

The gap between the general circumstances of the native black population of the United States, the descendants of Africans enslaved in the colonial era, and the native Indian population, and the general circumstances of the nonblack majority, the descendants of Europeans who migrated to this continent, is multi-dimensional, reaching far beyond differences in economic well-being. The gap directly influences prospects for the health and well-being of upcoming generations, for the sustenance of the spiritual and moral fiber of a people. The gap persists in the face of a host of changes: dramatic social policy initiatives such as the New Deal and the Great Society, the civil rights movement, periods of war and peace, and periods of prosperity and major depression.

There is a deep contradiction in the economics literature of the late 1970s and early 1980s over the post-civil rights economic progress of black America. When examined carefully this contradiction really indicates the opposing courses charted by the black underclass and the black middle class. For example, in 1973 Richard Freeman declared that there had been dramatic progress in the 1950s and especially in the 1960s, bringing blacks markedly closer to parity with whites in earnings. In fact, Freeman hypothesized that the trend toward "convergence in economic position...suggests a virtual collapse in traditional discriminatory patterns in the labor market" (p. 67). Freeman's declaration set the tone for a decade of research.

But in 1983 Freeman set the tone for the next decade's research with a far more somber message:

> The 1970s was a period of severe economic plight for inner-city black youth that went beyond the worst nightmares of even pessimistic social analysts. Rates of unemployment of young black men rose to unprecedented levels; labor participation rates fell; and as a consequence the ratio of employment to population plummeted to extraordinarily low levels. (p.67)

James Smith and Finis Welch (1989), while maintaining the position that blacks have made substantial strides economically over the past 40 years (due, they claim, to educational advance), conclude a recent paper with the following pessimistic note: "Unfortunately, there are also reasons for concern about the future, especially for the still large black underclass. . . ." (p.561)

In 1973 Freeman's attention was drawn to the elite strata of the black population, to evidence of its improved economic position—an improvement that directly led toward convergence in aggregate black-white earnings ratios. In 1983 Freeman's attention was drawn to the black underclass, whose economic position had stagnated, even deteriorated, since the civil rights revolution. In 1989 Smith and Welch see these two strata of the black population living economically disparate existences. The rosy reading of the aggregate data for the 1960s and 1970s was inaccurate, for most of the good news emanating from these sources was narrowly based, centering mainly on movements in black-white male wage and income ratios.

The economic situation of native blacks as a whole can in no way be sufficiently represented by shifts in the income and earnings of black males relative to white males. There are other important indicators that must be considered in order to portray the past and present economic conditions of blacks. But even the picture with regards to black male income and earnings has clouded over since the decade of the 1970s when Welch and Smith last took an in-depth look.

Utilizing data from the U.S. Bureau of Census' annual *Current Population Reports* we have found that the 20- to 24-year-old cohorts of 1967 to 1970, and the 25- to 34-year-old cohorts of 1967 to 1969, either improved or held on to their relative income positions over the next ten years. After 1980, however, this trend collapsed. With but one exception the relative incomes of the 20- to 24-year-old cohorts and 25- to 34-year-old cohorts of 1971 to 1974 had decreased ten years later over the 1981 to 1984 period. Black male workers who were 35 years and older in the late 1960s and mid-1970s also fared poorly over the next ten years. With but few exceptions their relative incomes were lower ten years later.

The early optimism of economists like Freeman and Smith and Welch did not reflect the full reality of white male-black male income disparities. Their conclusions were based upon data for year-round, full-time workers, and such workers among blacks are a smaller proportion of all income recipients than they are among whites. Moreover, while the proportion of full-time male workers has been declining for both groups, the decline in absolute terms for blacks has been greater than that for whites. In 1967, 53% of black male workers worked full-time, year-round, while for white workers the figure was 61.5%. By 1987 the black male proportion was about 5 percentage points lower, and the white male proportion was down 6 percentage points to 56.5%. The lowest point was 41.5% for black males in 1982 and 51.9% for white males during the same year.

A more telling measure of relative male incomes is the income ratio for all workers, both full- and part-time; full- and part-year. Generally, the absolute values of the median income ratios for all workers are lower than they are for full-time workers. Between 1967 and 1974, the average difference between the two ratios for workers of all ages was 8 percentage points. Between 1975 and 1987, the average difference increased to 12 percentage points. None of this affects the conclusions reached with respect to the decline in black relative incomes by age cohorts over the 1980s. Whether we use full-time data or part-time data the decline is still there.

To measure more accurately the economic reality for black males we include not only those with income but those without income. This requires using mean rather than median as the measure of average and correcting it for those who have been excluded because they had no income. This simple correction involves multiplying the mean by the proportion of the population with income. With such a correction we find the proportion of black males with income declined slightly over the 1967-1987 period, while the proportion of whites with income increased. In contrast to the median income ratios in Table 2-1, the mean income ratios are uniformly lower and the "corrected" mean income ratios lower still. Once again, the story is the same with respect to progress in this ratio. While the ratio for fully employed workers was higher in 1987 than in 1967 (.71 versus .64), and the ratio for all workers also was higher in 1987 than 1967 (.59 versus .57), the mean income ratio for those with and without income was an identical .55 in both years.

Expected payoffs in income relative to increased black male educational attainment also hit a snag during the 1980s. The black-white median income ratios for males 25 years and older in all schooling classes rose in the late 1960s and early 1970s. During the 1980s, however, the rates declined for all except those with four or more years of college. The decline was particularly pronounced among black high school graduates whose income relative to whites was the same in 1987 as in 1964. It would appear from this data that the relative income gains associated with increased educational attainments made by black males during the 1960s and 1970s have eroded in the 1980s.

Consider measures of the relative resources available to the black family. Two such measures, median family income and family wealth and asset ownership, also belie the claims of "dramatic" black economic advances. In 1967 the average black family had an income of $15,166 (in 1984 dollars) available to it, whereas the average white family enjoyed an income that was $10,450 higher at $25,616. Thus for every $1 of white family income black families had 59 cents. By 1984 the gap had grown wider. Black median family income in 1984 was $15,431, some $12,255 less than the $27,686 white families received. Now for every $1 of white family income black families had 56 cents. Moreover, white families fared much better than blacks in terms of real income growth. The black 1984 median family income was just $265 higher than the 1967 income; whites on the other hand enjoyed an increase of $2,070. And while black family income rose between 1967 and 1978, when it peaked at $17,321, so also did the difference rise between the amount of income available to whites and to blacks. This difference reached its peak in 1979 at $12,686. After 1978 and 1979, both black and white real income started to decline, but black income declined faster.

With respect to wealth, a census study using 1984 data found that the median net worth of a black family was $3,400, while that of a white family was 12 times as much at $39,000. Another way to look at it is that for every $1 in wealth held by a white family a comparable black family had 9 cents in wealth. For those families with incomes under $11,000 (the "official" poverty population), white families had 96 times greater net worth than blacks. White families with incomes between $11,000 and $48,000 (the broad middle class), had three to seven times more wealth than their black counterparts. White families with incomes in excess of $48,000 had twice the wealth of blacks in that category.

Finally, consider incomes of both black females and white females as compared with incomes of white males, the benchmark group. We report median income ratios for all workers as well as mean income ratios, corrected to include persons without in-

Table 2-1

Black-White Male Median Income Ratios for Year-Round,
Fully Employed Workers, by Age Cohorts, 1967-1987

Year	All Ages*	20-24	25-34 Total	25-29	30-34	35-44 Total	35-39	40-44	45-54	55-64
1967	.64	.68	.73	n.a.	n.a.	.61	n.a.	n.a.	.65	.57
1968	.68	.77	.71	n.a.	n.a.	.63	n.a.	n.a.	.68	.64
1969	.66	.80	.70	n.a.	n.a.	.66	n.a.	n.a.	.66	.62
1970	.68	.77	.72	n.a.	n.a.	.65	n.a.	n.a.	.67	.67
1971	.68	.86	.73	n.a.	n.a.	.63	n.a.	n.a.	.66	.60
1972	.68	.81	.72	n.a.	n.a.	.65	n.a.	n.a.	.63	.66
1973	.67	.79	.76	n.a.	n.a.	.68	n.a.	n.a.	.64	.62
1974	.70	.79	.80	n.a.	n.a.	.71	n.a.	n.a.	.67	.64
1975	.73	.83	.80	.85	.75	.72	.75	.69	.68	.71
1976	.72	.81	.79	.81	.76	.69	.70	.68	.66	.66
1977	.69	.84	.75	.77	.76	.74	.72	.75	.69	.60
1978	.77	.72	.86	.90	.84	.77	.81	.74	.69	.69
1979	.73	.79	.78	.77	.80	.76	.77	.75	.65	.66
1980	.70	.83	.76	.76	.78	.71	.70	.73	.64	.65
1981	.71	.82	.78	.82	.76	.68	.66	.69	.61	.66
1982	.71	.82	.77	.74	.79	.69	.73	.65	.64	.67
1983	.71	.74	.75	.75	.75	.76	.80	.75	.67	.60
1984	.68	.80	.72	.69	.73	.76	.82	.69	.67	.60
1985	.70	.79	.73	.69	.70	.70	.72	.69	.68	.68
1986	.71	.76	.73	.71	.73	.73	.73	.73	.71	.61
1987	.71	.79	.71	.75	.69	.76	.75	.78	.66	.65

*Includes persons 14 years and older in 1967-1978, and 15 years and older in 1979-1987.
Source: U.S. Bureau of Census, *Current Population Reports*, Series P-60, "Money Income of Households, Families and Persons in the United States," various years.

come. The latter ratios and those for all workers are quite similar. While all three statistics show that both black and white female incomes relative to those of white males have been on the increase since 1967, they also show how low those relative incomes were and still are. Among all workers a black female had an income that was only 25% as great as that of a white male in 1967. This proportion increased to 37% in 1984. If the black female was a year-round, full-time worker, her proportion went from 43% in 1967 to 57% in 1984. However, only 32 to 35% of black females in the labor force were year-round, full-time workers during the interval. "All workers" and "all persons" categories are more relevant for consideration of relative black female incomes. For the corrected mean relative income, the ratio rose in a manner similar to that for the "all workers" category, from .25 in 1967 to .38 in 1984.

The data in this report documents the laggard economic condition of the black family. But this condition is only one indicator of the scope of the crisis confronting America's native black population. To understand its full dimension requires a substantive historical inquiry into the evolving scheme of social relations in contemporary America.

The two-parent family has long been the norm in American society. Among the various racial and ethnic subgroups in the United States, the native black population has experienced the most drastic decline in the representation of this traditional family structure. The fraction of black families headed by women has grown from 25% in the 1950s to 50% in recent years. It is among this growing group of black families headed by mothers that poverty strikes hardest and most harshly. Single-parent status also appears to be correlated with a variety of disadvantages for children that extend far beyond the direct limitations imposed by poverty status. For example, a child from a single-parent family has a greater probability of dropping out of school. Although less well-documented, juvenile delinquency and early pregnancies have been attributed to the experience of growing up in single-parent families.

The growth of female-headed families among blacks is symptomatic of conditions that lie well below the surface of statistics, well below such catch-phrases as the "feminization of poverty." These phenomena are linked to the precarious status of black America as a whole in the current social milieu. The prevalence of black female-headed families is merely an indicator of an entire constellation of forces that negatively affect black Americans in our society.

The husband-wife family has always been relatively less the case among blacks than among other ethnic or racial groups in the United States. Slaveholders sought the breakup of family, tribe, and clan to individualize and subordinate the black population. Not until the mature period of slavery, when importation of Africans had all but ceased, did the slaveholders seek, in some cases, to promote more conventional family life amongst their slaves. The slaveholders' motives, of course, were commercial; they sought some measure of family stability to ensure a stable labor supply. The commercial value of the chattel was the dominant consideration, leading the slaveholders to buy and sell slaves without consideration for relational ties. From the outset, then, black family life was assaulted in America; indeed such assault was both fundamental to and a function of the system itself.

Emancipation led to feverish attempts by the freedmen to bring family members together; that was their first priority after slavery was brought to an end. However, many former slaves remained unattached to any family unit because no family members could be found. The post-reconstruction period was also characterized by an attempt on the part of the white aristocracy to regain control over black labor. The mechanism that restored many of the features of slave labor was the prison-lease system. Simultaneously, the prison-lease system contributed to the ongoing breakup of the black family by removing married black males from their families and by preventing unmarried black males from forming new families.

Largely confined to the unskilled categories of the national labor market, black male labor still was viewed as valuable, at least in a reserve capacity, by industrialists in the early twentieth century. Industrialists turned to black workers as strike-breakers, as a pool of available cheaper wage contestants in the labor market. The movement of black workers from the South to the urban North, in response to such calls for cheaper labor, led to additional familial dislocations.

Thus the forces undermining the black family from slavery times through the early part of the present century were consequences of attempts to utilize and control black labor—particularly black male labor—both within the slave system and the system that evolved after slavery. *But from the 1930s onward the forces undermining the black family increasingly have been associated with a perceived lack of necessity of black labor—especially black male labor.*

Whereas the conditions undermining the black family in the period prior to the 1930s were the character of capitalist development, largely within southern agriculture, since that time the conditions undermining the black family have been due to the development of a managerial society in the United States. Dominance by the business-financial elite in the United States gave way to dominance by the intellectuals and intelligentsia—the managerial class.

The principle guiding capitalist development was the profitable command of labor, both labor in use and labor in reserve (unemployed), but the principle guiding managerial development has been the scientific discharge of labor from the workplace, particularly manual labor. This pattern of discharge has meant the progressive marginalization of black males, long excluded from extensive participation in nonmanual and so-called "knowledge" occupations. Now large numbers of black males are faced with the elimination of the occupational categories for which they qualify. As the black male is moved further and further out to the margins of America's economy and society, this necessarily has repercussions for the black family.

The microelectronic-cum-robotics revolution has laid the groundwork for the elimination of a whole range of occupations, particularly manufacturing, without replacing those positions with new work. Capitalist development originated the process of continuous, albeit unsteady, reductions in labor time. This reduction generated a reserve of labor, a reserve that is disproportionately black in the United States.

This reserve–not employed but not unemployable–serves at least two functions: it provides employers with a ready pool of workers to draw upon during periods of rapid industrial expansion; and it serves as a restraint on the demands of unemployed workers. In contrast, for the managerial class this reserve of labor is without function. As the momentum of technical change renders labor superfluous, from a managerial perspective the "excess" population carried over from capitalist to postcapitalist society is genuinely unnecessary.

The position of the black male–and the black population in general–must be understood in the context of these broader trends and developments. Black males are overwhelmingly members of the working class, and in particular are represented in the inactive or surplus portion of the working class. Among their numbers are a large percentage of persons rarely employed, deeply entrenched in poverty, most likely to be imprisoned, most likely to be the military's foot soldiers–least likely to have a sense of optimism about the opportunities offered by American society. This segment of the black working class is referred to by sociologists as the black "underclass." Moreover, there is no evident place for them in the managerial age, as race and class harden into caste under circumstances where intergenerational social mobility becomes ever more elusive.

As the necessity for labor in the aggregate–particularly unskilled or low-skilled labor–continues to decline, the struggle to secure the remaining places on the occupational ladder will intensify. Racial and ethnic conflict will continue apace as groups seek to secure niches in the hierarchy of managerial society. In such an environment racial discrimination will continue, transmuted along new and more subtle lines by antidiscrimination legislation and litigation.

The dimensions of discrimination by race are vast, ranging from the exclusion of black youths from college preparatory tracks, to channeling black youths away from hard sciences, to outright exclusion from occupations. Particularly striking is the changing character of exclusion following the introduction of federal antidiscrimination measures. These measures did not address the power base of other ethnic contestants for occupational turf nor the incentives that exist for turf preservation. Only the decorative exteriors of discrimination were addressed, not the brick and mortar. The laws have merely produced new procedures to perpetuate exclusion. In their recent study on the structure of earnings, Taylor, Gwartney-Gibbs, and Farley (1986) find *no* sector of the U.S. economy that does not display significant discriminatory earnings differentials in the aftermath of antidiscrimination legislation.

In many different occupations, including jobs in the public sector such as in police and fire departments, the ascent of white workers up the seniority ladder was made easier because nonwhites were systematically excluded from competition for these jobs. Various union seniority systems were established at a time when racial minorities were barred from employment and union membership. Obviously blacks as a group, not just as individuals, constituted a class of victims who could not develop seniority status. A seniority system launched under these conditions inevitably becomes the institutionalized mechanism whereby whites as a group are granted racial privilege.

But in the unfolding managerial age it is necessary to look out for mechanisms and sites of exclusion other than those traditionally associated with union activity. In the age of science and technology it is the academy that assigns credibility, credentials, and the imprimaturs of authority. How do native blacks fare in obtaining access to quality institutions of higher education?

One could just as well ask how blacks fare in obtaining quality educational experience at all levels. The example of the city of Chicago is revealing. Nearly one-half of the students from Chicago's public schools do not finish high school, and this proportion is overwhelmingly black. Of course without a high school diploma a student is not even eligible for college admission.

The University of Illinois at Chicago (UIC), which enrolls primarily a regional undergraduate student body, has undergone an overall enrollment decline since 1979. But the decline in black student enrollment has been 40%, considerably more than the overall drop. Moreover, among black students actually matriculating the attrition rate is astonishing. Whereas 30.4% of white students entering UIC in the fall 1981 had graduated by 1987, only 7.4% of the black students had. For the class entering in 1982, while 25% of the white students had graduated by 1987, only 4.4% of the black students had done so.

The UIC case may be somewhat extreme but it is symptomatic of a national trend. At a major southern university, the University of North Carolina at Chapel Hill, black undergraduates experience academic suspension rates three times as high as those of white students.[1] The limited capacity of native blacks to gain from the academy and to influence the academy is also demonstrated by the drop in black enrollment in graduate schools. After peaking in the 1970s, the percentage of black graduate students has fallen from 5.1% in 1976 to 4.2% in 1982. Blacks remain a stable 4.6% of the professional school population. Sociologist Gail Thomas has offered the following explanations:

- The low quality of elementary and secondary schools in predominantly black areas channels black youths away from access to and interest in higher education.

- Guidance counselors fail to encourage black youths to pursue advanced degrees.

- The screening methods used to select students, given the traditionally poor performance of blacks on the SAT and the GRE, work against blacks, whose performance on such tests is hampered by test bias and the lack of early and adequate exposure to standardized tests.

Consistent with the broader themes of this report Thomas warns, "Blacks are at a dangerous point in terms of becoming disempowered as a result of what I see as a disturbing trend in higher education. . . " (Associated Press, 1987, p. 17A).

Blacks also are disappearing from the ranks of Ph.D. holders. Fields such as engineering, the physical sciences, and mathematics now consistently have less than 2% black representation among their doctorates. Between 1977 and 1987 the number of doctorates awarded to black American males declined by 54% from 684 to 317, lower than the absolute number awarded to Asian-American men in the same year.[2] The cumulative effect of negligible black representation in these fields is a complete dearth of black influence in the dissemination of knowledge, credentials, status, and authority. It reinforces the marginal status of the native black population in the era of science and technology.

Again with respect to the specific Chicago case, across all Chicago-area universities less than 3% of the faculties are black. Blacks are disproportionately untenured. It has been suggested that the lower tenure ratios for blacks are due to age (blacks on average are younger Ph.D. recipients) and due to the greater difficulty in obtaining tenure today. But the gap would persist even if the age distribution was the same, and even if tenure criteria had not stiffened, because a greater percent of blacks are on nontenure track appointments. For example, at UIC 32.7% of black and Hispanic faculty are not on tenure track compared with 17% of whites (Reis, 1987).

Further difficulties involve the concentration of black academics in history, sociology, and Afro-American studies. Moreover, less credibility is accorded research by black scholars doing racial research than is accorded white scholars. Black administrators, to a disproportionate degree, are not faculty members, making them more vulnerable to job loss if they take strong stands, less able to protect black faculty members faced with tenure denial. The fewer the blacks, the more prestigious the university. For example, in Chicago, while 14.9% of the faculty at Northeastern Illinois is black, only 2.6% of the faculty at Northwestern University is black (Reis, 1987).

The current trends seem locked in place, for the near term at least. Nationally in 1980-81 blacks received only 3.3% of undergraduate engineering degrees and a mere 1.6% of master's degrees. Less than 1% of engineering Ph.D.s were blacks. In 1980-81 blacks received 5.2% of the undergraduate degrees in biological sciences, largely from predominantly black schools, 2.9% of the master's degrees, and 1.7% of the Ph.D.s; blacks received 4% of the B.A.s in the physical sciences (also largely from black schools), 2% of the master's degrees, and 1% of the doctorates; in mathematics, blacks received 5.3% of the B.A.s (again largely from black schools), 2.6% of the master's degrees, and only 1.2% of Ph.D.s (Reis, 1987).

The American Council on Education estimates that American colleges and universities have 18,827 full-time black faculty, 4% of the total–a drop from 19,674 in 1977. Blacks constitute only 2.3% of the faculty at predominantly white institutions; 8,200 black educators are concentrated at 100 predominantly black college campuses, institutions with less resources, less prestige, and less influence than their white counterparts (Duvall, 1987).

The phenomenon of black exclusion from the academy is of special significance in the managerial age. It indicates how widely the social dimensions of discriminatory practices stretch. The relative absence of blacks from the academy begins with the differential in opportunities afforded by family resources and the differential in the quality of schooling in the early years; it continues with the deflecting of black college students from fields with greater technical requirements; and it concludes with the ghettoization of the residual of black academics in a handful of less-respected subfields of research. Ultimately blacks have negligible influence on the standards and procedures that govern access to the academy.

Antidiscrimination laws have not and cannot exercise much effect on these circumstances. Competition between ethnic and racial cliques produces the perpetuation of racial discrimination rather than its elimination. We are witnessing the historical outcome for the group that was always viewed by other (European) contesting groups as unworthy of entry into the ethnic social compromise over the allocation of occupational turf. Black workers consistently would be relegated to less-skilled jobs or denied jobs altogether. Matters only become worse when the range of available well-paid, blue-collar occupations narrow with structural change in the U.S. economy; after all, the discriminatory nature of the educational process inherently limits opportunities available to blacks.

Conclusions

Race continues to matter. Discrimination persists, although its forms have altered. The intrinsic nature of American society is geared toward ethnic/racial competition, the struggle to carve out social turf for one's own group. The conflict works itself out in the classic forms of American tribalism.

Blacks enter the turf wars with various disadvantages. Per capita income and wealth are comparatively low. Professional-level blacks frequently have supervisory or quasi-supervisory positions in social welfare administration, so that there is no significant basis for blacks to act independently of public sector "helping" positions. The relative deterioration of schooling, family life, health conditions, etc., all reinforce the disadvantages in ethnic/racial competition. And blacks have already lost many previous rounds of turf wars, since other contesting groups could all agree not to compromise with blacks. Class cleavages among blacks compound the difficulties in becoming successful competitors.

Familial and schooling crises are not uniquely black problems. These same symptoms of deterioration now appear among other groups. But among blacks these conditions are more acute and more visible, both anecdotally and statistically. And they layer on top of the inferior black position in America's ethnic/racial struggles.

If blacks are to be a healthy and contributing presence in the United States, the options are straightforward. Either the compromise must finally be struck, formally or informally, and native blacks granted an appropriate set of positions in managerial society's social structure, or a struggle must be waged against the structure itself. The former route means blacks must opt fully for a representative share of the general (rather than merely racial) equality. The latter route means a far more radical course of action and would require calling into question the values that produce success in our competitive and hierarchical society.

I have touched upon the most troubling prospect of all: that a continued black presence is by no means assured. For in the transitition from capitalism to managerialism those relegated to the surplus population will find their very existence threatened. In fact, to the extent that *blacks* are viewed as the social problem, and hence objects of social management, rather than the *system* being viewed as the social problem, the danger should be clear. What is happening in black America today merely foreshadows the full force inherent in the rise of the managerial estate. Not only will the question "Who needs the Negro?" be voiced with greater frequency, but the question "Who *is* needed and who *is* not?" will be applied broadly across the entire population. The answers are likely to be as chilling as the question.

Notes

1.   Data obtained from the University of North Carolina at Chapel Hill.

2.   See D.K. Magner's article "Decline in Doctorates Earned by Black and White Men Persists, Study Finds; Foreign Students and U.S. Women Fill Gaps," published March 1, 1989 in *The Chronicle of Higher Education*. In the same article, C. Smith, Dean of Graduate Studies at Florida A & M University, is quoted as observing that "The black male appears to be in a dangerous state of decline in both academics and society."

References

Associated Press. (1987, December 29). Black Enrollment in Graduate Schools Drop, Study Says. *Durham Morning Herald.*

Duvall, J. (1987, October 31). New Organization Seeks to Be Voice of Black Professors. *The Carolina Times,* pp. 1, 4.

Freeman, R.B. (1973). Changes in the Labor Market for Black Americans, 1948-72. *Brookings Papers on Economic Activity 1.*

Freeman, R.B. (1983, August 11-12). *Who Escapes? The Relation of Church-Going and Other Background Factors to the Socio-Economic Performance of Black Male Youths from Inner-City Poverty Tracts.* Paper prepared for the National Bureau of Economic Research Conference on Inner-City Black Youth Unemployment, Cambridge, MA.

Reis, D. (1987, May). Minorities on Slow Tenure Track at Chicago Area Universities. *Chicago Reviewer*, pp. 3-5.

Smith, J.P., & Welch, F. (1986, February). *Closing the Gap: Forty Years of Economic Progress for Blacks*. Santa Monica: The Rand Corporation.

Smith, J.P., & Welch, F. (1989, June). Black Economic Progress After Myrdal. *Journal of Economic Literature, 17* (2), 561.

Taylor, P.A., Gwartney-Gibbs, P.A., & Farley, R. (1986). Changes in the Structure of Earnings Inequality by Race, Sex and Industrial Sector, 1960-80. *Research in Social Stratification and Mobility, 5*, 105-38.

U.S. Bureau of the Census. (1983a). *Characterization of the Population Below the Poverty Level: 1981* Current Population Reports Series P-60 No. 137. Washington, DC: U.S. Government Printing Office. P. 8.

U.S. Bureau of the Census. (1983b). *Money Income of Households, Families and Persons in the United States; 1981*. Current Population Reports Series P-60 No. 137. Washington, DC: U.S. Government Printing Office. P. 102.

3

Research on African-American Families: A Holistic Perspective

Robert B. Hill

The impressive social and economic gains of black families during the 1960s were severely eroded during the 1970s and 1980s. Between 1969 and 1983 the jobless rate among all blacks soared from 6% to 20%–the highest level ever recorded for blacks by the U.S. Labor Department. Officially, the jobless rate for blacks fell to 12% by 1988, but unofficially, a depression-level one out of four black workers are unemployed.

Both two-parent and single-parent African-American families were affected by this record-level unemployment. Four back-to-back recessions between 1970 and 1985 led to a tripling in the jobless rates among husbands and wives in two-parent families and among women heading single families. Black youths also experienced sharp increases in joblessness. Between 1969 and 1983, unemployment among black teenagers doubled from one-fourth to one-half. Although officially the jobless rate for black teens fell to one-third by 1988, unofficially it is again a different story: three out of five black youths are unemployed.

Soaring unemployment and double-digit inflation led to sharp increases in poverty. While the proportion of black families in poverty edged up from 28% to 30% between 1969 and 1987, the number of poor black families soared from 1.4 million to 2.1 million. Increasing economic instability among African-American families contributed to many social problems: family instability, adolescent pregnancies, school dropouts, welfare recipiency, ill health, drug abuse, alcohol abuse, delinquency, crime, homelessness, child neglect, and family violence.

While most low-income African-American families experienced increased economic and social deprivation during the 1970s and 1980s many middle and upper-middle black families made important gains. But because this generally occurred among black families with two earners, the gains were dependent on a new and in many ways unsettling feature of family life. The worsening circumstances of low-income black families has become a widely-discussed issue. And hundreds of black organizations at the national and local levels have assigned top priority to initiatives to enhance the social and economic functioning of African-American families.

Conventional Perspective

Unfortunately, the conventional perspective accepted by large segments of the news media and by social scientists and policymakers is "the deficit model," also known as "blaming the victim." This perspective has contributed to a widespread lack of understanding of the causes and nature of the contemporary situation of African-American families. The "deficit model" has the following features:

- It attributes the problems of black families to internal "defects," such as single-parent families, "a culture of poverty," lack of work orientation, low educational achievement, poor work ethic, welfare mentality, etc. A recent manifestation of the "deficit" perspective was the CBS-TV documentary produced by Bill Moyers in January 1986, which characterized female-headed black families as "vanishing" nonfamilies and attributed most of their problems to family structure.

- It concentrates on the most disadvantaged subgroups of black families and depicts them as representative of the majority. For example, although poor female-headed families on welfare comprise only 16% of all black families living in poverty areas, most commentators continue to characterize such "underclass" families as representing the overwhelming majority of black families residing in poverty areas.

- It fails to focus on positive coping strategies, cultural patterns, and self-help networks among African-American families. For example, the national focus on the black "underclass" deflects attention from the significance of the black "working class." The conventional perspective is unbalanced, since it deemphasizes or omits entirely any careful examination of positive features of African-American families, such as extended families, bicultural socialization, child-rearing practices, etc.

- It deemphasizes the contribution of current racism to the social and economic ills afflicting black families. For example, according to the thesis of the declining significance of race, class is a more important determinant of black life-chances today than race. But this thesis fails to assess the impact of institutional racism. The conventional perspective treats African-American families in a superficial, fragmented, and peripheral fashion; and it applies ad hoc, arbitrary explanations that have not been derived from systematic theoretical formulations and have not been supported by empirical evidence.

Holistic Perspective

The social and economic functioning of African-American families can best be enhanced through research strategies and policy initiatives that are based on an "holistic" framework in which families are the central unit of analysis. Almost a century ago, at the meetings of the American Academy of Political and Social Science, Du Bois (1898), set forth a holistic framework for studying black people. He argued that proper understanding of American blacks could not be achieved without assessing the role of historical, cultural, social, economic, and political forces. Unfortunately, Du Bois' recommendations to employ a holistic framework in analyses of black individuals and families have not been heeded by mainstream social scientists–even after 90 years. The recent study of black Americans by the National Research Council (1989) reflects this continuing failure of American social science.

This report will: (1) examine recent social and economic trends among black families; (2) describe how the holistic framework enhances understanding of the nature, causes, and cures of the current crisis among black families; (3) assess the impact of external and internal factors on black families; (4) highlight new research that facilitates the development of effective strategies for strengthening black families; and (5) offer recommendations to public and private policy makers and to service providers and self-help institutions in the black community to enhance the viability of African-American families.

Recent Social and Economic Trends

To understand changes in the structure and functioning of African-American families during the 1970s and 1980s, the following economic trends need to be considered: employment patterns, occupational patterns, racial income gap, real income patterns, poverty trends, welfare patterns, noncash benefits, and child support. These trends in turn are closely related to: single-parent families, out-of-wedlock births, child care, informal adoption, foster care, formal adoption, child abuse, and housing.

Employment Patterns

Heads of both two-parent and one-parent families are strongly affected by unemployment. The number of unemployed black husbands rose from 84,000 to 188,000 between 1969 and 1985, while their jobless rate more than doubled from 2.9% to 7.1%. In 1969 only 38,000 (5.6%) black women heading families were unemployed. By 1985 273,000 female heads of black families were unemployed, while their jobless rate tripled to 16.4%.

Income Shifts

As the number of low-income African-American families increased, the number of middle-income and upper-income black families also rose. While the proportion of poor black families rose from 28% to 30% between 1969 and 1987, the proportion of black families with incomes of $25,000 or more increased from 33% to 36% and the proportion of black families with incomes of $50,000 and over increased from 6% to 10%.

Single-Parent Families

The number of single-parent families increased 50 times faster among college-educated black women (+496%) between 1970 and 1985 than among black women who failed to complete high school (+10%). Despite their higher educational attainment, black women heading families were three times more likely to be unemployed in 1985 (16.4%) than they were in 1969 (5.6%). Black women heads of families are disproportionately poor—not because they do not have husbands but because they do not have jobs. Only one out of four employed women heading black families is poor, compared to three out of four unemployed black women heading families.

Out-of-Wedlock Births

Sharp increases in out-of-wedlock births contributed to the rise in single-parent black families. The surge in out-of-wedlock births among blacks and whites during the 1970s resulted from the unprecedented number of young women of child-bearing age as a result of the post-war "baby boom." Although out-of-wedlock births have been declining recently among black teenagers, black teens are still four times more likely than white teens to have children out-of-wedlock. Moreover, inadequate health care and nutrition increase the risks for these black babies of dying in infancy or having a low birth weight. And high dropout rates increase the chances of adolescent mothers being unemployed and going on welfare.

Housing Patterns

The lack of affordable housing has become increasingly acute for working-class and poor families. Although home ownership in the U.S. reached a record high of 66% in 1980, by the third quarter of 1985 it had plummeted to 64%—its lowest level since 1968. Home ownership rose from 65% to 68% among whites between 1970 and 1980, and from 42% to 44% among blacks.

The housing crisis will become more severe for low-income black families. Although the number of poor households is projected to grow from 11.9 million to 17.2 million between 1983 and 2003, the number of low-income housing units is projected to shrink from 12.9 million to 9.4 million. Moreover, about half a million low-income units are disappearing each year, largely due to widespread displacement of poor families as a result of urban renewal, abandonment, gentrification, and condominium conversions.

The housing shortage for the poor is directly responsible for the sharp increases in homelessness. While HUD estimated the homeless population in the U.S. at 250,000-300,000 in 1984, advocates for the homeless contend that it is closer to 2-3 million. One-third of the homeless consists of families with children. In addition, there are hundreds of thousands of "couch people," families who double-up with relatives and close friends for varying periods of time. Concerted national action is needed to prevent the problem of homelessness from worsening for African-American families during the 1990s.

A Holistic Perspective of Black Families

Comprehensive Frameworks

One of the most significant efforts to incorporate Du Bois' holistic framework for studying black families was undertaken by Billingsley. Based on the structural-functional theory of the family posited by Parsons and Bales (1955), Billingsley (1968) was the first scholar to adapt the systems framework for the study of black family life. His paradigm depicted black families as a social subsystem mutually interacting with subsystems in the black community and with subsystems in the wider white society.

Moreover, to reflect the structural diversity of black families, Billingsley developed a topology depicting 32 kinds of nuclear, extended, and augmented family households. This topology underscores the fact that the structure, functioning, and needs of black families may change significantly as family members pass through various stages of their life cycles. Unfortunately, the important research and policy implications of Billingsley's systems framework and family topology have not been adequately explored by social scientists over the past two decades.

According to Allen (1978), a major weakness of the structural-functional approach was its static character. He urged the incorporation of developmental concepts into the systems framework so that families could be viewed dynamically.

Blocked Opportunity

One theoretical perspective that many scholars have found useful for explaining stress and coping behavior among blacks is Merton's (1957) theory of anomie and deviance, also known as the blocked opportunity theory. According to this thesis, high rates of deviant behavior are expected among groups who are frustrated in achieving societal goals (e.g., monetary success) through legitimate means (e.g., education or employment) because of class and racial barriers. Merton's blocked opportunity paradigm enhances our understanding of black families when it is combined with Billingsley's system framework and Allen's developmental approach.

African-American Culture

Many other scholars have offered useful Afro-centric frameworks for understanding black families. For example, Nobles (1974) has consistently argued that no significant advance in our knowledge of black families will occur until social scientists recognize them as *African-American* families; and Karenga (1982, 1986), along with other scholars, has made a persuasive case for placing analyses of black families within a cultural framework.

There is a vital need for research on the relative merits of these various theoretical paradigms in addressing issues about the separate and combined effects of social forces and social policies–at the community, family, and individual levels–on black family structure and functioning. The holistic perspective that we recommend to guide research and policy development related to African-American families combines the systems, developmental, blocked opportunity, and cultural frameworks. This holistic framework will facilitate the identification issues that need to be addressed for an understanding of the nature, causes, and remedies of problems affecting black families. Most of these issues are either ignored or deemphasized in the deficit model.

Integrating concepts from the systems, developmental, blocked opportunity, and cultural paradigms, the following two operational questions will guide the presentation of this report: (1) "What do we know about the extent to which societal forces, social policies, community subsystems, family subsystems, and individual factors impede or facilitate the functioning of African-American families?"; and (2) "What implications does this knowledge have for developing policies in the public and private sectors, and for developing self-help strategies in the black community, that will improve the social and economic well-being of low-income and middle-income black families?" We shall first examine the negative and positive effects of societal forces, social policies and factors. Then we shall recommend action by public and private policy makers and by service providers and self-help institutions in the black community.

Impact of Societal Forces

The major societal forces that have adversely affected African-American families over the past two decades are: racism, classism, sexism, back-to-back recessions, double-digit inflation, the shift from high-paying manufacturing jobs to low-paying service jobs, and increased job competition from legal and illegal immigrants.

Institutional Racism

The fundamental weakness of the declining racism thesis is its focus on individual racism, its failure to systematically assess the role of institutional racism. As Carmichael and Hamilton (1967) observed, institutional racism may be overt or covert, intended or unintended. Covert discrimination involves the deliberate mistreatment of minorities by organizations or institutions based on nonracial criteria that are strongly correlated with race. Such discrimination is also known as "patterned evasion," the deliberate use of proxies for race in order to deny equal opportunities to racial minorities. The grandfather clauses, literacy tests, and poll taxes are early examples of patterned evasions in the area of voting rights.

Structural Discrimination

A major impediment to the development of strategies to counteract the effects of institutional racism on black families has been the failure to recognize or acknowledge the role of unintentional, or structural, discrimination. Unintentional institutional discrimination refers to the consequences of societal forces or policies which, though not designed to be discriminatory, have adverse effects on racial and ethnic minorities.

Society-wide trends such as recessions, inflationary spirals, the closing of plants in inner-cities, automation, and shift from manufacturing to high-tech and service industries, have had unintended, discriminatory effects on black families. Such structural discrimination has contributed to persistently high rates of "structural unemployment" among young and adult workers in black families.

Sexism

Sexism is a major societal force for perpetuating the subordination of women to men. Although white women also persistently encounter sexism, such experiences by black women have more devastating effects on black families. For one thing, black women are much more likely than white women to head single-parent families and to be the primary breadwinners in those families.

Since black families headed by women are popularly characterized as "matriarchal," "vanishing," "non-families," "pathological," and "broken," they experience discrimination in may areas: employment, housing, bank loans and credit, health, adoption and foster care, social welfare, the administration of justice, etc. Wives in black families are more likely than wives in white families to experience sexual discrimination in the labor market. Black women are also more likely to hold low-paying "traditionally female" occupations than are white women. And black women experience disproportionate levels of mental and physical abuse from black men, who experience more institutional barriers and frustrations than do white men.

Impact of Social Policies

Black families are disproportionately affected by social policies: fiscal and monetary decisions, income and payroll taxes, block grants, budget cuts in programs for the poor, welfare, child support, foster care and adoption, housing, plant closings in central cities, job training programs, and unemployment insurance.

Fiscal and Monetary Policies

The four most recent presidents–Nixon, Ford, Carter, and Reagan–promised not to place the burden of fighting spiraling inflation on the backs of the unemployed. Nevertheless, the four back-to-back recessions during the 1970s and 1980s were the results of their respective monetary policies; they were not "natural disasters." Traditionally, the Federal Reserve Board stems inflation by keeping interest rates within predetermined ranges, while permitting the money supply to expand more freely. These restrictive fiscal policies produced the recessions of 1970-71 and 1974-75.

Soaring interest rates led to the 1980 recession and similar tight money policies brought on the 1981-82 recession–the most severe decline since the Great Depression. These spiraling interest rates also contributed to the disproportionate failures of black businesses, less able than white businesses to obtain commercial loans at affordable rates. Federal fiscal and monetary policies during this period had an acute adverse impact on black workers, families, and businesses.

Block Grants

Although block grants are invariably omitted from most policy analyses of black families, the transforming of categorical grants to block grants during the 1970s and 1980s contributed significantly to the shifting of government resources from blacks and low-income groups to middle-income groups. President Nixon's "New Federalism" combined many Great Society programs into "revenue sharing" block grants. Model Cities was replaced by the Community Development Block Grant (CDBG), the Manpower Development and Training Act (MDTA) by the Comprehensive Employment and Training Act (CETA) manpower block grant, and Title IV-A by the Title XX social services block grant.

Since block grants have little federal oversight and do not distribute monies primarily on the basis of economic need, many suburban areas with low levels of unemployment and little substandard housing or poverty received sizable CETA, CDBG, and Title XX funds. Several high-level evaluations revealed that minorities and other economically disadvantaged groups benefited less from the decentralized block grants of the 1970s than they did from the centralized categorical programs of the 1960s.

Reagan Budget Cuts

Most cuts in programs for the poor during the Reagan administration tightened eligibility requirements for the working poor and at the same time reduced the value of cash and noncash benefits for the poor who did receive assistance. The OBRA cuts in 1981 removed between 400,000-500,000 working poor families from the welfare rolls and eliminated about one million persons from the food stamps program. About 300,000 working poor families who remained on AFDC experienced sharp reductions in cash and in-kind benefits because of increased work disincentives.

Welfare Policies

The government policies most often cited as a major cause of black family instability are those related to welfare, especially the Aid to Families with Dependent Children (AFDC) program. According to conventional wisdom, the surge in female-headed families and out-of-wedlock births among blacks during the 1970s and 1980s was caused mainly by the increasing availability of AFDC. However, comprehensive reviews of research findings by Wilson and Neckerman (1986), Ellwood and Bane (1984) and Darity and Myers (1984), found no credible evidence for popular assumptions about welfare causality. Most of these reviews concluded that black male unemployment and the shortage of marriageable men were more strongly associated with black female-headed family formation than the "attractiveness" of welfare benefits.

Housing Policies

At the same time that the FHA mortgage program (established in 1934) subsidized the large-scale exodus of whites to the suburbs, it confined blacks—regardless of income—to central cities. Moreover, urban renewal policies undermined the stability of black families and businesses in many low-income communities. Working-class and poor black families have been displaced from their homes and communities by urban renewal, highway construction, housing abandonment, escalating rents, excessive property taxes, condominium conversions, and gentrification. Yet most studies of black family instability fail to examine the impact of public and private housing policies.

Impact of Community Subsystems

The features of many inner-city communities that have a significant adverse impact on black families include persistent high rates of unemployment, crime, delinquency, gang violence, drug abuse, AIDS, and alcohol abuse. Counteracting these, there are many self-help institutions, such as churches, fraternal groups, voluntary associations, schools, neighborhood groups, and extended family networks, all of which represent and support the vitality and resilience of African-American families.

Joblessness

Joblessness has devastating ramifications throughout the black community. Not only is persistent unemployment likely to lead to poverty, but since most jobless black breadwinners are not eligible for unemployment benefits, they are often forced to turn to welfare. Moreover, as Brenner (1976) and other researchers have shown, high rates of unemployment are correlated directly with high levels of alcoholism, wife abuse, child abuse, family break-ups, mental illness, physical illness, suicides, crime, and imprisonment.

Crime

As many classic studies of crime have documented, groups with the highest rates of unemployment also have the highest rates of crime. Consequently, blacks are overrepresented in arrests, convictions, and incarceration. While blacks comprise 12% of the U.S. population, they account for one-fourth of arrestees and one-half of state prisoners. The "crack" epidemic has led to record-level increases in crime, homicides, and gang violence in black communities. Such disproportionate rates of arrests, convictions, and incarceration contribute to the formation of black single-parent families.

Self-Help Institutions

Numerous studies have found that mediating structures (such as churches, voluntary associations, fraternal groups, extended family networks, etc.) provide the bulk of the services received daily by individuals and families. The overwhelming majority of black people will turn to their informal support network before turning to formal support systems (social workers, doctors, lawyers, etc.). For example, since 85% of black teenager mothers live in three-generational households with their own parents or other adult relatives, most of the social and economic support they receive each day is provided by their immediate family and kin—not by welfare or other government agencies.

Black Churches

Black churches currently provide a wide range of social services that strengthen families and enhance positive development of children. Services provided include day care, pre-school programs, nurseries, support to single parents, parenting, family counseling, remedial education, family planning, drug abuse prevention, job training, and recreational activities. More recently, church-based mentoring and rites-of-passage programs have been developed to prepare black males for manhood and fatherhood. As a result of the Father Clement's "One Church, One Child" program, black churches across the nation have launched initiatives to find permanent homes for black children who are in foster care.

To offset the declining availability of low-income housing in inner-city areas, more and more black churches are building affordable housing for low-income families and senior citizens. Moreover, to revitalize entire neighborhoods, black churches have formed community development corporations to increase the stock of affordable housing and to stimulate black business development. Stronger empirical documentation of the broad array of services provided by black churches will be provided as a result of the Black Church Family Project, directed by Andrew Billingsley at the University of Maryland at College Park. This national survey of family support programs is one of the most comprehensive investigations of outreach programs by black churches ever undertaken.

Fraternal Organizations

Many fraternal groups in black colleges are providing important services and support to low-income families. In 1984, Delta Sigma Theta Sorority launched Summit II, a comprehensive program to assist black single mothers. Similarly, Alpha Phi Alpha Fraternity formed "Project Alpha" to provide male role models for young black males in single-parent families. Many other black fraternal groups provide services to families and children in inner-city areas.

Voluntary Associations

Voluntary associations have always provided major support to black families. As Du Bois noted, women's clubs have been in the vanguard of such efforts. These women's groups formed orphanages, nursing homes, nursery schools, elementary schools, hospitals, and businesses. National black women's self-help groups that continue to perform important family support functions include: National Council of Negro Women, National Black Nurses Association, Jack and Jill of America, the Links, National Hook-Up of Black Women, the Coalition of Black Women, and the National Black Women's Health Project. Since 1986, the National Council of Negro Women has been sponsoring Black Family Reunions in the nation's capital as well as in many cities across the nation.

The two oldest voluntary black associations that have provided support to black families are the National Urban League (NUL) and the NAACP. To mobilize the resources of black national organizations to address the problems of African-American families, the NUL and NAACP cosponsored the Black Family Summit at Fisk University from May 3-5, 1984.

Impact of Family Subsystems

Most studies of African-American families have concentrated on two family characteristics–structure and social class. But the focus on family structure has been dichotomous–one-parent or two-parent. Thus the broad range of nuclear, extended, and augmented household structures of black families has been largely ignored. The focus on social class has also been dichotomous–either underclass or middle-class. This simplistic dichotomy obscures the importance of understanding conditions among the working-class–which represents the plurality of black families. Moreover, in-depth analyses of the role of African-American cultural patterns, including coping strategies and self-help efforts, is minimized in or omitted from traditional studies.

Family Functioning

Conventional studies of black families also fail to clearly operationalize the concept of family "functioning." Although Billingsley (1968) identified three types of family functions–instrumental, expressive, and instructional–these distinctions have not been adequately utilized. Instead it is customary to generalize about functioning solely on the basis of structure; to assume that inadequate functioning in one domain (e.g., economic) is generalizable to other domains (e.g., child-rearing); and to generalize about dynamic processes based on static, cross-sectional data. The most common practice is to equate family functioning with family structure. One-parent families are arbitrarily assumed to be "broken" and "unstable," while two-parent families are assumed to be "intact" and "stable"–without providing any independent assessment of the stability or cohesion of each type of family.

Family Culture

Another concept that is widely distorted in most analyses of African-American families is that of culture. This term is often used synonymously with society and class. This intermingling of concepts is manifested in the following deficiencies: the denial of any African cultural legacy; the popular acceptance of a "culture of poverty"; and the failure to define operationally African-American cultural patterns. Contrary to the conclusions of the NRC study, many contemporary cross-cultural studies have identified Africanisms in contemporary black life, such as the extended family, child-rearing patterns, religion, language, music, art, rituals, nutrition, health, etc.

Extended Families

As the NRC study exemplifies, sweeping assertions about the decline of extended families among blacks are made without providing any supporting empirical data. Yet many studies reveal that kinship networks continue to provide vital social and economic support to African-American families. Nine out of ten babies born out-of-wedlock to black teenagers live in three-generational households. Although the proportion of extended family households remained at 11% among whites between 1970 and 1980, the proportion of extended family households among blacks rose from 23% to 28%. The number of black children living with kin increased from 1.3 million to 1.6 million between 1970 and 1987 and the proportion of black children in informally adoptive families rose from 13% to 17%.

The Impact of Individual Factors

Culture of Poverty Norms

According to conventional wisdom, conformity to "culture of poverty," "lower-class," or "underclass" norms, values, and beliefs is considered to be a major determinant of black family ills. The NRC study and many other investigations have found no empirical support for popular notions of distinct "culture of poverty" norms, values, and beliefs among low-income blacks. Proof of distinct "subcultures" among low-income blacks would require evidence of homogeneity of values, attitudes, and behavior patterns. Yet empirical inquiries have revealed, on the contrary, much heterogeneity in these patterns among poor black families. In short, while low-income blacks may share a common economic status, they are not monolithic in their values and attitudes, their aspirations and lifestyles.

Dysfunctional Attitudes

While some analysts do not point to a distinct "poverty culture" as the primary factor responsible for "self-perpetuating" the problems of black families, they identify negative psychological attitudes, such as lack of self-esteem, lack of sense of efficacy, achievement, and future orientation. Low-income persons tend to score significantly lower on psychological measures of efficacy, achievement, and future orientation than do middle-income and upper-income persons–regardless of race. However, a major shortcoming of these studies is that they are overwhelmingly based on cross-sectional surveys that obtain measurements at only one point in time.

In order to provide a more adequate test, Duncan and his colleagues at the University of Michigan incorporated several attitude measurements into their national representative Panel Study of Income Dynamics (PSID). More specifically, changes in the economic status of male- and female-headed households between 1971 and 1978 were related to three attitudinal measures: achievement motivation, orientation toward the future, and a sense of personal efficacy (e.g., control over one's life).

Extensive analysis by the University of Michigan researchers (Duncan & Morgan, 1981; Duncan, 1984) revealed that having "good" or "bad" attitudes was not significantly related to whether one went into or out of poverty. For example, persons with high achievement orientation and sense of efficacy were just as likely to fall into poverty (or rise out of it) as those with low achievement orientation and sense of efficacy. They concluded that negative life events (such as unemployment, illness, divorce or separation, unwanted pregnancy or birth, eviction, etc.) were more important determinants of downward economic mobility than psychological disposition.

Action Implications

This report contends that the nature and causes of the current crisis among black families cannot be properly understood without incorporating a holistic perspective that systematically examines the separate and combined effects of social forces and social policies–at the community, family, and individual levels–within systems, within developmental and cultural theoretical frameworks. Societal forces with an adverse impact on black families include: racism, classism, sexism, back-to-back recessions, double-digit inflation, shift from higher-paying manufacturing jobs to lower-paying service jobs, and increased job competition from legal and illegal immigrants. Black families were also adversely affected by social policies in such areas as: employment, plant closings, taxes, trade, monetary supply, welfare, foster care, child support, housing, health, education, and criminal justice.

Major negative factors at the community, family, and individual levels include: joblessness, poverty, crime, delinquency, drug abuse, alcohol abuse, AIDS, family violence, child neglect and abuse, mental illness, physical illness, homelessness, out-of-wedlock births, adolescent pregnancies, low educational attainment, poor work skills, work discouragement, low self-esteem, and other dysfunctional attitudes. At the same time, numerous self-help institutions in the black community (such as churches, social action organizations, fraternal groups, neighborhood groups, and extended family networks) have helped many African-American families to counteract negative forces at the societal, community, and family levels.

The crisis will not be resolved without holistic strategies undertaken in both the public and the private sectors. Fortunately, comprehensive agendas for strengthening black families have been proposed by many groups in and outside the black community. Some of our key recommendations are as follows:

Stimulating Economic Growth

Most analyses reveal that an expanding economy contributes significantly to economic progress among black families and that it is possible to reduce racial inequality while pursuing economic growth. Consequently, the black community must insist that government policies to reduce inflation no longer rely on raising unemployment by inducing recessions. Moreover, since small businesses generate the largest numbers of new jobs in the American economy, more government resources and set-asides should be targeted to enhancing the effectiveness of small businesses, especially those operated by minority entrepreneurs.

Achieving Full Employment

This nation must rededicate itself to the goals of the Employment Act of 1946 and the Humphrey-Hawkins Act of 1978–to provide everyone willing and able to work with jobs at liveable wages. Current tax credits that subsidize the exporting of American jobs abroad should be reversed to provide greater incentives for creating jobs at home. Moreover, liveable wages will not be achieved until the federal minimum wage, which has remained at \$3.35 an hour since 1981, is raised to a level (\$4.50 or thereabouts) to restore its traditional purchasing power. And job training programs should give higher priority to women heading low-income families and to adolescent parents–male and female.

Expanding Child Care

A major barrier to the labor force participation of many black women is the lack of affordable child care. Unfortunately, the current Dependent Care Tax Credit (DCTC) is not used by most working poor parents, since their incomes are too low to produce tax liabilities. Consequently, the DCTC should be made "refundable," similar to the Earned Income Tax Credit (EITC), to insure that working poor families receive tax rebates for child care–even when they do not have to pay taxes. Moreover, this nation should give serious consideration to implementing a children's allowance, similar to those provided in many European countries.

Reforming AFDC

The Family Support Act of 1988 contains several provisions to help welfare recipients achieve economic self-sufficiency: the ineffective WIN program was replaced by JOBS–a comprehensive education, training, and employment program; states guarantee child care for welfare mothers required to participate in JOBS; child care and Medicaid coverage are extended for 12 months for families of recipients who leave welfare rolls due to employment; and the AFDC-Unemployed Parent (AFDC-UP) program is mandated for all 50 states.

However, genuine reform should provide more: mandating periodic AFDC increases; establishing minimum AFDC needs and payment standards; raising the ceiling for AFDC eligibility to the poverty level; abolishing the 100-hour ceiling and prior work criteria for AFDC-UP eligibility; and assigning high priority to enhancing basic skills and job training for low-income and young noncustodial fathers.

Enhancing Child Support

The 1988 Family Support Act more effectively enforced child support collections by establishing efficient procedures for establishing paternity, locating absent parents, and withholding wages and tax refunds. Nevertheless, many inequities continue to exist in current child support policies: inadequate levels of court-awarded child support; sharp disparities between amount of child support payments and ability to pay; premature termination of families from AFDC; difficulty working poor families have in obtaining child support services; and policies that force low-income noncustodial fathers to pay higher proportions of their income for child support than middle-income fathers. In order to eliminate such deficiencies, more comprehensive and equitable approaches are needed, such as the Child Support Assurance program currently being tested in the state of Wisconsin.

Reforming Foster Care

Unfortunately, most proposals to reform the welfare system omit entirely the foster care system—despite the fact that long-term foster care youths have the highest risk of becoming welfare recipients, delinquents, and criminals. The number of children in foster care, especially among blacks and Hispanics, spiraled during the 1980s as a result of sharp increases in unemployment, poverty, drug abuse, homelessness, and AIDS. However, innovative grassroots efforts such as Homes for Black Children and "One Church, One Child" have found more than enough black families to provide for children in need of foster care or formally adoptive homes. Foster care policies should be reformed to strengthen extended family networks by providing higher reimbursements to relatives than to nonrelatives in adoptive placements.

In addition to forming citizens' foster care monitoring groups, the black community should insist that minority-operated community groups with a demonstrated record for finding homes for "hard-to-place" children be licensed to place special needs black children and to provide comprehensive family preservation and other preventive services. It is important that such groups not be restricted to recruiting black foster care or adoptive families for nonminority agencies.

Enhancing Public Housing

Public housing residents in many cities have demonstrated they can manage their housing facilities more cost-effectively than local government agencies, at the same time reducing markedly the level of welfare dependency. For example, in Washington, D.C., Kenilworth-Parkside's Residence Management Corporation has created about a dozen small businesses operated by public housing residents, has sent over 500 of its youth to college, and has reduced unemployment, welfare dependency, adolescent pregnancy, and drug abuse. Public housing resident councils in other cities should be provided with appropriate technical assistance so that they may assume greater control of their housing facilities.

Expanding Low-Income Housing

The increasing unavailability of affordable housing for low-income families has led to a surge in overcrowding, homelessness, foster care placements, child neglect, family violence, physical illness, and mental illness. Vigorous lobbying efforts are needed to expand the availability of subsidized rental units, to restore thousands of units of abandoned and boarded-up housing, and to expand home ownership options for low-income families, such as urban homesteading, "self-help," and "sweat equity" housing.

References

Allen, W.R. (1978). The Search for Applicable Theories of Black Family Life. *Journal of Marriage and the Family, 40*(1), 117-129.

Billingsley, A. (1968). *Black Families in White America.* Englewood Cliffs, NJ: Prentice-Hall.

Brenner, M.H. (1979, October 31). Pathology and the National Economy. U.S. Congress, Joint Economic Committee, Task Force on Economic Priorities.

Carmichael, S. & Hamilton, C. (1967). *Black Power.* New York: Vintage Books.

Darity, W.A. & Myers, S.L., Jr. (1984, November). Does Welfare Dependency Cause Female Hardship: The Case of the Black Family. *Journal of Marriage and the Family,* 765-779.

Du Bois, W.E.B. (1898, January). The Study of the Negro Problem. *Annals, 1,* 1-23.

Duncan, G.J. (Ed.). (1984). *Years of Poverty-Years of Plenty: The Changing Economic Fortunes of American Workers and Families.* Ann Arbor: Institute for Social Research, University of Michigan.

Duncan, G.J. & Morgan, J.N. (1981). Sense of Efficacy and Subsequent Change in Earnings: A Replication. *Journal of Human Resources, 16*(4), 649-657.

Ellwood, D.T. & Bane, M.J. (1984). The Impact of AFDC on Family Structure and Living Arrangements. U.S. Department of Health and Human Services.

Karenga, M. (1982). *Introduction to Black Studies.* Los Angeles, CA: Kawaida Publications.

Karenga, M. (1986, October). Social Ethics and the Black Family: An Alternative Analysis. *The Black Scholar, 17*(5), 41-54.

Merton, R.K. (1957). *Social Theory and Social Structure.* Glencoe, IL: The Free Press.

National Research Council. (1989). *A Common Destiny: Blacks and American Society.* Washington, DC: National Academy Press.

Nobles, W. (1974). African Root and American Fruit: The Black Family. *Journal of Social and Behavioral Sciences, 20*(2), 52-63.

Parson, T. & Bales, R.F. (1955). *Family, Socialization and Interaction Process.* Glencoe, IL: Free Press.

Wilson, W.J. & Neckerman, K. (1986). Poverty and Family Structure. In S. Danziger & D.H. Weinberg (Eds.), *Fighting Poverty: What Works and What Doesn't.* Cambridge, MA: Harvard University Press.

4

Black Political Participation

E. Yvonne Moss

Black political participation in the period 1940 to the present has taken both conventional and nonconventional forms. Until the Voting Rights Act of 1965 secured the franchise for millions of black Americans in the South and in some jurisdictions in the North and West, black political participation was necessarily unconventional, typically taking the form of protests and political movements. These protests and demonstrations played a pivotal role in the political and social advancement of black Americans. The election of black public officials in urban America would not have been possible without the foundation provided by political movements. Any review of the trends in black registration and voting makes it clear why black Americans could not rely upon conventional political methods.

Voting

The Supreme Court ruling that the white primary was unconstitutional (*Smith v. Allwright*, 1944) paved the way for a 140% increase in black voter registration in the South between 1940 and 1947 (see Table 4-1). Between 1960 and 1964, during the height of the civil rights movement, black registration increased by 34%. Another large increase, 73%, followed the passage of the Voting Rights Act of 1965 (see Table 4-1).

An examination of registration rates by states in the South indicates an overall increase of black registration from 35.5% just before passage of the Voting Rights Act of 1965 to 57.2% immediately following passage of the act (see Table 4-2). Yet large gaps remain between nonwhite and white registration rates even after 1965. Although the registration rate of whites in all southern states increased only minimally from 73.4% to 76.5%, in five of the eleven states whites were registered at a rate approximately 30% higher than blacks. In one state, Tennessee, the percentage of increase in white voter registration was greater than that for blacks.

In presidential elections, black voter registration remained relatively stable between 1968 and 1984. With white registration rates dropping in presidential elections from 75.4% in 1968 to 69.3% in 1980, rebounding slightly to 69.6% in 1984, the ratio of black to white voter registration nationally increased from 88% to 95%, an appreciable convergence.

Table 4-1

Black Voter Registration in the South, 1940-1973

Year	Estimated Number of Registered	Percentage of Black Voting Age Population
1940	250,000	5
1947	595,000	12
1952	1,008,614	20
1956	1,238,038	25
1960	1,414,052	28
1964	1,907,279	38
1968	3,312,000	62
1970	3,357,000	54
1971	3,488,565	59
1973	3,560,856	59

Source: "Black Politics in the South," by D. Campbell and J.R. Feagin, 1975, *Journal of Politics, 37*, p. 133.

Table 4-2

Voter Registration in the South, Prior to and After the Voting Rights Act of 1965

State	Pre-Act Registration Percentage		% Point Difference*	Post-Act Registration Percentage		% Point Difference*
	White	Nonwhite		White	Nonwhite	
Alabama	69.2	19.3	49.9	89.6	51.6	38.0
Arkansas	65.5	40.4	25.1	72.4	62.8	9.6
Florida	74.8	51.2	23.6	81.4	63.6	17.6
Georgia	62.6	27.4	35.2	80.3	52.6	27.7
Louisiana	80.5	31.6	48.9	93.1	58.9	34.2
Mississippi	69.9	6.7	63.2	91.5	59.8	31.7
North Carolina	96.8	46.8	50.0	83.0	51.3	31.7
South Carolina	75.7	37.3	38.4	81.7	51.2	30.5
Tennessee	72.9	69.5	3.4	80.6	71.7	8.9
Texas	....	....	....	53.3	61.6	-8.3
Virginia	61.1	38.3	22.8	63.4	55.6	7.8
Total	73.4	35.5	37.9	76.5	57.2	19.3

Source: *Political Participation* (pp. 222-23), by U.S. Commission on Civil Rights, 1968, Washington, DC: Government Printing Office.

*Prepared by author.

When voter turnout rather than registration is examined the increases among black Americans are again dramatic (see Tables 4-3 and 4-4). In presidential elections black voter turnout hovered around 33% in the 1950s. It increased to 52.9% in 1960, to 64.9% in 1964, and it has remained relatively stable from that date to the present. In the South voter turnout among black citizens increased from 4% in 1952 to 31% in 1960 and to 63% in 1968.

In presidential elections, it appears from available data that African-Americans voted overwhelmingly Democratic between the years 1940 and 1948. This trend has continued through to the present. Black citizens voted overwhelmingly for Democratic candidates between 1952 and 1984 (see Table 4-5). The year in which the lowest support for Democratic presidential candidates was recorded was 1956, when 64% of the black electorate voted Democratic.

The increases in black participation in electoral politics should be viewed within a political context in which there have been major barriers to registration and voting. In the years 1940 through 1987, there were five types of barriers to full participation in electoral contests: legal or procedural barriers, illegal barriers, socioeconomic barriers, psychological barriers, and organizational barriers. Legal or procedural barriers include pre-1965 mechanisms, such as the white primary, poll taxes, and literacy tests, which resulted in disfranchisement. Since 1965, other methods have been used to discourage registration and voting among African-Americans: difficult registration requirements, frequent purges of registration rolls, moving polling places with little or no notice, reducing the number of polling places within black residential areas.

Dilution refers to that set of devices and strategies used to minimize the potential impact of black political participation. Methods used to dilute black electoral potential include at-large elections, gerrymandering, anti-single shot devices, annexation of predominately white areas to an electoral jurisdiction, and run-off elections requiring no less than 50% of the vote. Numerous examples illustrate the particular effectiveness of at-large elections in diluting black voting strength. In Texas in the 1970s, the number of African-Americans and Mexican-Americans elected under ward systems was three times higher than the number elected under previous at-large systems. After the passage of the Voting Rights Act of 1965, in at least 20 counties, many in the South, jurisdictions changed from district to at-large elections. In southern states covered by the preclearance provisions of the Voting Rights Act there was a positive relationship between the number of black elected officials and the number of requests for changes of electoral procedures, including at-large elections, annexations, and changes in polling places. Often states enacted such changes without preclearance. When these preclearance requests were turned down, some jurisdictions implemented them anyway.

Before 1965 a number of illegal methods were used to bar black citizens from voting. These included terror, economic and physical harm, verbal abuse, and arbitrary registration procedures. Such tactics were concentrated in 129 counties in ten southern states. Since 1965 a number of illegal devices are still employed to keep black

Table 4-3

National Registration and Voting by Race, 1964-1984

	1964	1968	1972	1976	1980	1984
Blacks						
Percentage of voting-age population reported registered	NA	66.2%	65.5%	58.5%	60.0%	66.3%
Percentage of voting-age population reported voting	58.5%	57.6%	52.1%	48.7%	50.5%	55.8%
Whites						
Percentage of voting-age population reported registered	NA	75.4%	73.4%	68.3%	68.6%	69.6%
Percentage of voting-age population reported voting	70.7%	69.1%	64.5%	60.9%	61.1%	61.4%

Source: *Current Population Reports, Special Studies*, U.S. Bureau of the Census, Series P-23, No. 131.

Table 4-4

Reported Voter Turnout by Race for Presidential Elections, 1952-1984

	1952	1956	1960	1964	1968	1972	1976	1980	1984
White	78.5	76.5	81.9	79.6	77.1	73.8	72.5	72.3	75.2
Black	33.1	34.9	52.9	64.9	67.7	64.7	65.0	66.7	65.6

Source: Data for 1952 to 1978 from *American National Election Studies Data Sourcebook, 1952-1978* (p. 317), by W.E. Miller, A.H. Miller, and E.J. Schneider; 1980, Cambridge: Harvard University Press. Data for 1980, 1982, and 1984 from American National Election Studies, Center for Political Studies, University of Michigan.

Table 4-5

Percent Democratic Vote in Presidential Elections, 1952-84

	1952	1956	1960	1964	1968	1972	1976	1980	1984
Blacks	80	64	71	100	97	87	95	86	91
Whites	40	39	48	65	41	30	47	36	33

Source: Data for 1952 to 1976 from *American National Election Studies Data Sourcebook, 1952-1978*, by W.E. Miller, A.H. Miller, and E.J. Schneider; 1980, Cambridge: Harvard University Press. Data for 1980 to 1984 cited in *The Social Basis of Politics* by A.K. Sherman and A. Kolker, 1987, Belmont, CA: Wadsworth.

Americans from exercising their right to vote. Arbitrary registration procedures continue to be a problem. Posted hours are not kept; polling places are illegally changed; voter rolls are illegally purged; and black voters are subject to various kinds of harassment, such as losing the names of black Americans on the voting list.

Contrary to conventional wisdom about the relationship of socioeconomic status (SES) and voting, black citizens with low SES are more likely to vote than whites with low SES. It is primarily structural factors which influence black voter turnout. The most important is the "political climate," whether the electoral structure is supportive, intolerant, or indifferent to black political participation. Black voters turn out in higher numbers regardless of SES when they have something or someone to vote for and when structural factors are not a barrier.

It is not clear what role psychological factors such as fear, apathy, and deference to whites—which historically had an impact of black voting pattern—have today. Organizational factors, however, are clearly related in various ways to black registration and voting. The reluctance of political parties to nominate and support black candidates for office has a negative effect on black participation. On the other hand, the presence of black candidates and federal registrars is significantly related to black political mobilization. In city races, the presence of black mayoral candidates increase black voter turnouts. In presidential politics, Jesse Jackson's bid for the Democratic nomination significantly increased black registration and voting. In Alabama, there was an 87% increase; in New York, the increase was a dramatic 127%.

Historically, there evolved in this country a political culture that legitimized the exclusion of black Americans from the political process. Black people lost more than the right to vote. What was also lost were the political benefits that derive from suffrage rights. These rights include opportunities for employment, education, and services. In 1880 black Americans were a majority in 300 counties in the United States. By 1970 that number was down to 100. Imagine the impact on black life, on the life of the nation, if political inclusion rather than political exclusion had been the norm in American politics from the 1880s onward.

Electing Black Officials

The impact of black registration and voting during the years 1940 to 1987 has been considerable. Yet controversy continues over whether greater participation in politics can change the material conditions of most African-Americans. The Voting Rights Act of 1965 created the opportunity for millions of black people to register and vote without harassment, threats, or fears of reprisals. This accomplishment is of historical importance. Black Americans began to enjoy some of the benefits of citizenship for the first time in the nation's history. Black voters have helped to elect blacks to public office as well as whites sympathetic to black interests. For example, even though black elected officials (BEOs) represented only 1.2% of the total number of elected officials in the U.S. (490,770) in 1984, there was a 300% increase in the number of BEOs between 1970 and 1985, from 1,469 to 6,065 (see Table 4-6). While there were fewer than 500 BEOs in the country before 1965, by 1988 there were 6,289. These gains, however, are not reflected at all levels of government. The greatest inroads have been at the county level. The election of black candidates to statewide offices has been the least successful. Thus, Virginia's election of a black governor was especially historic. There are no black representatives in the U.S. Senate and but a few in Congress. There is one governor and a very few statewide officials. This situation has led some scholars to conclude that electoral success has not placed black Americans where they can exercise real power.

In recent years the number of BEOs has declined. Since the most critical determinant of electoral success is the percentage of blacks voting in a district–the election of BEOs in districts with black people representing less than 40% of the population is not common–the number of blacks elected to office would seem to be limited by the number of majority or near-majority black districts there are in the U.S. However, the presence of black voters has an impact even when black officeholders are not elected. The presence of black voters affects the political agendas of white candidates and officeholders. For example, there was a marked decline in the segregationist rhetoric in southern gubernatorial races after the increase in black voter participation. And white members of Congress with a sizable black population in their districts have supported civil rights legislation.

While the election of black officials, even big-city mayors, has done little to reduce the overall economic inequality between blacks and whites, BEOs have had positive impact on the distribution of employment. For example, there has been an increase in the proportion of black municipal employees. Some argue that increases in black municipal employment primarily benefits members of the black middle class. The power of city government to affect social change has decreased because of changes in urban political structures. Black mayors are not able to provide the benefits to their constituents that ethnic mayors in political machines were traditionally able to provide. Participation does not bring the power it once did to effect social mobility.

What is clear is that black voters are becoming more sophisticated in utilizing the vote as a political resource, rewarding friends and punishing enemies whether black or white. Though over 6,209,000 black Americans remained unregistered in 1987, the gap between voter registration rates for black and white citizens narrowed from 9.2% in 1968 to 3.3% in 1984 (see Table 4-3). The gap in voter turnout narrowed from 10.6% in 1980 to 5.6% in 1984 (see Table 4-3). The steady increase in the numbers of BEOs since 1965 is likely to continue even with the limited number of majority black districts. Such increases are conditioned on prospects for black candidates capturing larger shares of the votes of other racial groups, including whites; increases in black voter registration and turnout; and whether structural barriers that effect political participation among African-Americans are reduced.

Critical contributions to the successful candidacies of black Americans have been made by black churches and community organizations. They provide the per-

Table 4-6

Change in Number of Black Elected Officials by Category of Office, 1970-1985

Year	Total	Federal	State	Substate Regional	County	Municipal	Judicial/law Enforcement	Education
1970	1,469	10	169	--	92	623	213	362
1971	1,860	14	202	--	120	785	274	465
1972	2,264	14	210	--	176	932	263	669
1973	2,261	16	240	--	211	1,053	334	767
1974	2,291	17	239	--	242	1,360	340	793
1975	3,503	18	281	--	305	1,573	387	939
1976	3,979	18	281	30	355	1,889	412	994
1977	4,311	17	299	33	381	2,083	447	1,051
1978	4,503	17	299	26	410	2,159	454	1,138
1979	4,607	17	313	25	398	2,224	486	1,144
1980	4,912	17	323	25	451	2,356	526	1,214
1981	5,038	18	341	30	449	2,384	549	1,267
1982	5,160	18	336	35	465	2,477	563	1,266
1983	5,606	21	379	29	496	2,697	607	1,377
1984*	5,700	21	389	30	518	2,735	636	1,371
1985	6,056	20	396	32	611	2,898	661	1,438

*The 1984 figures reflect blacks who took office during the seven-month period between July 1, 1983 and January 30, 1984

Source: *National Roster of Black Elected Officials*, Joint Center for Political Studies, 1985, Washington, DC: Government Printing Office.

manent infrastructure of black political movements. Astute black politicians have used community organizations combined with social and fraternal organizations as sources for the mobilization of black citizens. The theory of comparative advantage is used to explain the different roles various community groups have played in political movements and electoral campaigns. Groups like the Urban League and the NAACP reach their established clienteles. Political activists target new clientele groups. Black newspapers and radio stations keep the message alive. Social and fraternal organizations along with black churches spread the message, solicit volunteers, and raise funds. Churches provide arenas wherein groups with different goals and orientations come together to create working relations. Churches also function as intermediaries for political parties. Black churches act as centers for political mobilization, sometimes for specific campaigns, sometimes on a continuous basis. Political leaders have historically been recruited and developed from the black clergy, and black ministers have played significant roles in electoral politics and in programs for economic development.

Black ministers have, for example, provided access for politicians to their congregations, have mobilized church members for mass protests or electoral politics, have run for political office themselves or acted as power brokers for others. A significant example of this is evident in the campaigns of the Reverend Jesse Jackson for the Democratic party nomination for president in 1984 and 1988. His candidacy was one of the most striking new political developments in American politics in recent years. For the first time the possibility of an African-American president began to be taken seriously.

Black participation in presidential and local political campaigns have provided interesting information about how to activate the "unmotivated" voter. "Unmotivated" voters are mobilized to participate in politics because of the potential for success of a candidate or cause and because the process itself encourages the development of a sense of personal empowerment. And there is group motivation as well as individual motivation. Political movements, products of incremental political experiences, prepare potential voters for political activity. The protests of the 1960s, for example, moved people from passive to active participation. While African-Americans still lag behind Euro-Americans in lobbying activities, black registration and voting rates are now roughly equivalent to white rates. In terms of certain activities in election campaigns, African-Americans have higher rates of participation than Euro-Americans. Scholars note that the policy choices and attitudes of black citizens who do not vote are quite different from those who do. It is not entirely clear what these differences are. It is clear that there is growing black participation in politics, especially at the local levels.

Black Public Opinion

There has been widespread speculation that one significant change in black politics over the last few years has been a growing conservatism among black Americans, especially those ranked as middle class, a group that has grown from approximately 5% in 1955 to 33% in 1985. Evidence does not support this speculation. Few reliable studies of black opinion have been published. An examination of these published studies yields the following insights. Using the two traditional ways of measuring ideological preference, self-identification and reaction to specific issues, researchers found that relatively few blacks consider themselves to be conservative. Only 15% of those interviewed in a 1984 Gallup/Joint Center for Political Studies poll placed themselves on the three most conservative positions on a 10-point scale. Thirty-four percent placed themselves on the three most liberal positions.

Additionally, in reaction to social welfare issues (Should the government spend more money on health, education, welfare, and social issues?), black respondents were more liberal than white respondents at all income levels. The liberal gap was greatest among respondents with higher incomes. On race issues, black citizens were more favorable than white citizens on busing, affirmative action, and government spending to help African-Americans. There are few studies of black opinion on abortion and school prayer issues. From what is available on black attitudes on morality issues, African-Americans are more conservative than Euro-Americans on mandatory school prayer, abortion, and women's rights (except ERA). However, blacks are more opposed to the death penalty and more likely to favor gun control than whites. For black citizens, ideological self-identification and issue positions are not related even for persons at higher income levels. For example, black people who identify themselves as conservative are as likely to take liberal positions on social welfare spending as black liberals.

What is clear from the available fragmentary data is that patterns of public opinion among African-Americans do not fit easily into the traditional typologies used to explain patterns of Euro-American public opinion. When comparing intraracial ideological patterns it appears that members of the black middle class are more conservative on social welfare issues than black citizens with lower SES, but less conservative on race and morality issues. In the overall spectrum of American politics, middle-class blacks are quite liberal. On racial issues the black middle class is not more conservative than lower classes. On moral issues, there is no evidence that members of the black middle class are overall more conservative than members of the black lower class. With regard to gender differences, black women are more likely to vote Democratic than black men and are more opposed to military spending, yet there are no significant gender differences on issues of social welfare, morality, and affirmative action. In short, there is not much evidence of a new black conservatism.

Power, Exclusion, and Black Politics

Until 1965 the basic thrust of black political efforts was a search for power, i.e., a struggle to influence the decisions that affected black lives. Disfranchisement, dilution, and the structure of racial politics were major barriers to the acquisition of power. Black citizens turned to both conventional and nonconventional politics to overcome this politics of exclusion.

Even after dramatic increases in black participation in conventional politics and electoral victories, the search for power by African-Americans continues because of the limits of constitutional government, political change in governmental structures, and the overall structure of power in American. As the salient concern shifted from whether black Americans would be allowed to participate in the political system, to what the terms of that participation would be, to the consequences of participation, one of the most important issues was whether black political activity could lead to improvements in economic and social status of African-Americans.

There are inherent limits on the exercise of power within the political system. The structure of private power influences public decision making in significant ways. The contemporary challenge for black politics, then, goes beyond the capture of elective office and conventional political participation. The larger challenge concerns effective representation of black interest in all significant arenas of policy formulation. There is a need for public debate of the political options available to move blacks from a politics of exclusion to one of inclusion. A politics of inclusion resurrects the moral dimensions of American politics and moves towards a true sense of democracy in which citizens not only have a right to vote, but also influence over decisions that affect their lives.

Conclusion

An evaluation of the participation of African-Americans in the political life of the nation since the 1940s indicates a tremendous upsurge in voter registration and turnout, especially in the aftermath of the passage of the Voting Rights Act of 1965. Black participation in presidential elections indicates a narrowing gap between participation rates of blacks and whites. Increased participation has meant that elected officials have become more sensitive to black needs when the interests of Afro-Americans and Euro-Americans converge. Old problems remain and new issues surface as the possibilities of political activity are explored and as the limitations of such activity are exposed: how to manage ethnic and racial group relations; how to manage interracial conflicts; how to keep black elected officials accountable to their constituencies; and how to maximize the interests of black citizens within the constraints of the political system.

5

Blacks, A Valuable National
Pool of Talent

Charles V. Willie

Editorial note: The articles mentioned throughout this summary appear in Volume III of the Assessment of the Status of African-Americans series entitled *Education of African-Americans*.

Review and Analysis

Historian Meyer Weinberg, in an article entitled "The Civil Rights Movement and Educational Change," states that the significance of the modern version of this movement is that blacks have taken control of its leadership. Improved education for blacks was a major goal of the movement, and Weinberg agrees with Martin Luther King, Jr.'s assessment that the public policy for educational change "was written in the streets" through demonstrations, marches, and acts of civil disobedience. The legal strategy of the civil rights movement, again according to Weinberg, was to challenge the inherent inequity of a dual system of education—one system for whites and the other system for blacks, separate and unequal.

After this system was declared illegal in the courts, concern for equity and equality slacked, leaving, in Weinberg's view, an unfinished agenda, especially in large cities where schools are so underfunded that they provide an inadequate education for all students, black and white. Urban education issues, Weinberg believes, must be addressed, and at a higher level of priority.

In "Black Higher Education Demographics," Reginald Wilson identifies that sector of the education system where he believes equal opportunity has been experienced the least, the colleges and universities. His research reveals that as recently as 1941, according to a survey by the Julius Rosenwald Fund, there were only two tenured black professors employed full-time by predominantly white colleges or universities in the United States. He describes the bicentennial celebration of this nation (1976-77) as the peak year for minority enrollment in higher education; but since that time, accelerating during the 1980s, the proportions of minorities in colleges, graduate schools, and institutions for professional education have declined. Like Weinberg, Wilson attributes educational progress for blacks and other minorities, in part, to civil rights laws—the laws that, in King's words, were "written in the streets." As demonstrations for justice have decreased, so have the proportions of blacks and other minorities enrolled in college and universities.

Wilson's analysis is straightforward. He states that "college enrollment for minority groups is related to family financial status" and that the "cost of higher education continues to represent a barrier to poor black and Hispanic students." One need not look to cultural, psychological, or genetic factors to explain the underenrollment of blacks and other minorities in higher education. The poverty of black people limits their capacity to educate their children. When resources external to family finances are available to them, more blacks go to college. The GI Bill and Pell Grant are two such funding sources cited by Wilson.

Blacks who do manage to cross the threshold of institutions of higher education tend to enroll in less expensive and less prestigious schools. Four to five out of every ten undergraduate blacks in higher education are enrolled in a two-year community college. More than one-quarter of all bachelor degrees awarded to blacks are awarded by historically black colleges and universities. Blacks are prevented from enrolling in many colleges and universities because of restrictive admissions policies. Many blacks are limited because of their income to the few institutions that welcome the poor.

In addition to assisting in the completion of educational reform in elementary and secondary schools called for by the civil rights movement, public as well as private colleges and universities should respond appropriately in their admissions procedures. According to Weinberg, the public schools began but did not complete the task of eliminating racial inequality, root and branch. And, higher education, as indicated by Wilson, only half-heartedly and for a short period of time launched programs of inclusion that offered blacks and other minorities a fair share of seats in entering classes.

Whites have been and continue to be disproportionately represented in the student bodies of colleges, universities, and graduate professional schools. Blacks have been and continue to be disproportionately represented in two-year community colleges and in four-year institutions established for members of their race. Wilson explains these phenomena by way of a simple calculus: When the American society was generous with grants and scholarships for blacks and other minorities, their number and proportion in all colleges and universities increased; when such financial aid was withdrawn, the proportion of minorities in higher education decreased. Culture-of-poverty constructions, with their assertions of intergenerational transition, are inadequate explanations for the lower incidence and prevalence rates of blacks and other minorities in the colleges and universities of this nation. Their inadequacy is pointed up by Wilson's simple calculus.

The limited assistance that blacks have received to improve their educational status during the second half of the twentieth century has been, as mentioned earlier, a stop-and-go process. In effect, blacks forced the nation to pay attention to them when they decided to cease cooperating in their own oppression. The article that I have entitled "Case Study of Philanthropic Assistance" about the Rockefeller Foundation is a contribution to the discussion of this thesis.

On December 1, 1955, Rosa Parks was arrested in Montgomery, Alabama, for refusing to give up her seat on a city bus to a white person, as required by the law. Some characterized this brave act and the support that Rosa Parks received as the beginning of the "black revolt." Blacks, in their reaction to this event, sent a message to whites that the age of passive subservience had ended.

Challenges to inequality in other sectors of society escalated and led to the 1963 March on Washington, where Martin Luther King, Jr., a college-educated black minister, delivered the historic speech about his dream of freedom and justice in America. The nation responded. That year, for example, the Rockefeller Foundation designed and implemented a new program that was called the Equal Opportunity Program.

The actions of the Rockefeller Foundation are particularly appropriate to observe because of that foundation's historic interest in the education of blacks. Initial grants in the new program were designed to open the doors of "good schools" to minority candidates. To implement the program, several awards were made to prestigious, predominantly white colleges. The Rockefeller Foundation was struggling to make an appropriate response to the "black revolt." However, its efforts in the early 1960s were conditioned by habits of yesteryear. Support was given largely to predominantly white institutions because the foundation wanted to attract black students into the mainstream. Predominantly black colleges and universities were not recognized by the establishment as the mainstream.

Blacks found certain students, faculty, and administrators in these "mainstream" schools to be insensitive, insulting, and untrustworthy. Some blacks felt that the Rockefeller Foundation's recruitment program for these predominantly white schools was an invitation to a briar patch rather than to a rose garden. Estrangement increased between black students and white students on several white college campuses. The hoped-for racial reconciliation did not materialize.

The foundation modified its Equal Opportunity Program during the mid-1960s and included some predominantly black colleges as grant recipients. But the grants that were made to such schools were not comparable to the larger sums that had been offered to predominantly white colleges. Nevertheless, this modest midcourse correction indicated that the white establishment was becoming sensitized to feelings in the black community that whites tended to discount the value and legitimacy of their institutions in the new drive toward racial integration.

The Rockefeller Foundation began to internalize these new learnings. It consulted more and more with predominantly black institutions of higher education. It turned toward these institutions as a partner rather than as a patron. Slowly but surely the Rockefeller Foundation changed its focus from the paternalist rescue of selected black individuals to the fostering of institutional change in society on terms that were acceptable to blacks. This was a commendable shift.

However, the foundation discovered that it was unprepared for this new thrust. The absence of blacks on its staff was both a source of embarrassment and a liability for an organization that was determined to change its old ways of doing business, determined to relate to minorities in new and different ways. The experience of a homogeneously white staff was too narrow to correctly interpret the needs of blacks. As the 1960s decade closed, the foundation diversified its staff and broadened its mission so that the Equal Opportunity Program could bring minorities into the "mainstream" and could sponsor activities designed to effect institutional change in society.

The trials and tribulations of the Rockefeller Foundation during the 1960s decade were not unlike those of other predominantly white, establishment-oriented institutions. New occasions were teaching new duties. But, as we have already seen, these new learnings did not immunize establishment leaders, especially those in education, against the possibility of backsliding. All of this is to say that there is no linear pattern of progress in the attainment of educational equity. With two steps forward there is sometimes one step backward. Nevertheless, the educational innovations and changes of the 1960s were real and of value. The United States was set on a course unlike any it had pursued before. And while it might digress from time to time, the mood of minorities would prevent a return to the old paternalistic ways of offering help to people of color.

If the responses to the arrest of Rosa Parks in Montgomery and the March on Washington were significant events that contributed to changes in the way that whites related to blacks in the United States, the assassination of Martin Luther King, Jr., in Memphis in 1968 was a decisive event. King was an articulate, well-educated, and cosmopolitan minister who advocated a nonviolent approach to social change. His murder was experienced as the ultimate form of rejection. After the death of King, many whites in America, including some in charge of major institutions, realized that the racial prejudice that they had harbored was a form of social pathology that harmed whites as well as blacks.

Blacks realized that in King they had presented their best. If he was unacceptable, none could aspire to be acceptable. After the death of King, blacks saw with increasing clarity that they were rejected in this society not because of their behavior but because of their race. The Rockefeller Foundation understood this as well as any white-dominated organization, and in 1969, the year after Martin Luther King, Jr., died, it deliberately adopted a goal of diversifying its staff. In effect the Rockefeller Foundation and other institutions in the United State recognized that they must root out racial discrimination within their own organizations so that they could offer genuine help to others.

By confessing their faults, the people of power were acknowledging that, in the past, they had been self-centered rather than other-concerned. Their altruistic activity, including educational philanthropy, was orchestrated primarily to fulfill the needs of the helpers, and only secondarily the needs of those helped. Before King was killed, many whites in America believed that their way of life should be the model for all and that minorities should conform to white norms.

One indication that this nation was learning a new way was the increased school desegregation activity of the 1970s. The midpoint of this decade was the peak period for the enrollment of blacks in higher education and also the height of public school desegregation. In an article entitled "The Future of School Desegregation," I assert that "school desegregation has contributed to the enhancement of education in this nation probably more...than any other experience in recent years." Among the benefits of school desegregation have been the decline in the school dropout rate for black students and the increase in high school graduation rate for all students. Desegregation, not segregation, was the expectation of the 1970s. Public opinion polls revealed that seven out of every ten black parents "preferred" an "integrated" school for their children and that seven out of every ten white parents "would not object" to a "desegregated" education for their children.

As noted earlier, backsliding is an ever-present possibility. At the end of this decade, blacks again had been denied; their expectations and preferences had not been fulfilled. Court-ordered desegregation seldom desegregated black schools. Actually, the whites who usually were the defendants in desegregation court cases experienced more school desegregation than the blacks who usually were the prevailing plaintiffs. In Atlanta, Milwaukee, St. Louis, and other communities, court-sanctioned school desegregation plans prohibited any all-white schools but permitted several all-black schools. Since school desegregation was a beneficial experience and contributed to many school improvements such as magnet schools, bilingual education, and other innovations, the people in power hoarded these plums for their own kind.

Initially, school desegregation in this nation was conceptualized largely as a student experience. Little attention was given to integrating local education authorities such as school boards. Since self-interest is the basic motive for human action, these white-dominated decision-making bodies fulfilled the interests of whites and granted all of their children a desegregated education while denying such education to a substantial proportion of black students. I have visited school districts throughout the nation and heard superintendents under court order to desegregate ask the question, "How many one-race schools will the court let us get away with?" Despite such attitudes, I maintain that "school desegregation...has been the greatest contribution in this century to educational reform" and that it deserves to continue, with appropriate modifications, so that its promises are fulfilled for black and other minority students, indeed for all students.

Increasingly, blacks realized during the concluding years of the 1970s that some court-ordered school desegregation plans could be legal but still unfair. As the 1980s began, blacks had two contrasting reactions. Some embraced desegregation, others rejected it, outraged by persisting inequities in many court-ordered plans. On balance, more blacks favored desegregation than opposed it, as indicated in Meyer Weinberg's article, "Black Parents and Their Schools." The major complaint had to do with the burden of desegregation falling inequitably upon blacks. Thus, blacks who were against inequitable desegregation were not against an equitable integration.

A major concern of these blacks was the need for systemic rather than cosmetic change. Merely mixing and matching children by race was considered educationally inadequate. James Comer and Norris Haynes explain in their article, "Meeting the Needs of Black Children in Public Schools," that the academy must take into consideration the special needs of blacks and other population groups. Unwittingly, the schools to date have dealt largely with the normative behavior and needs of affluent whites. By fashioning an educational program that addresses the problems of dependency, powerlessness, and the absence of group control which often characterize the black experience in the United States, Comer and Haynes believe that educational outcomes can be significantly changed. In New Haven, a program that was designed with the black experience in mind, "empowered parents, teachers, administrators and students through collaborative, cooperative, coordinated planning in a few schools." The program created "a climate of relationships in which there is mutual respect among all...in the educational enterprise."

In essence, the program described by Comer and Haynes focused on relationships as well as basics. The relationship factor, they believe, is of paramount importance. Using traditional test-score measures of outcome, the New Haven program worked beautifully. Schoolchildren that followed the Comer model out-achieved other schoolchildren. Moreover, the program helped students become responsible adult members of a democratic society. Comer believes that the New Haven experience can and should be replicated elsewhere.

Faustine Jones-Wilson indicates why the Comer model has not been widely replicated. She states in an article entitled "School Improvement Among Blacks: Implications for Excellence and Equity" that urban school improvement has not been a national priority, especially during the 1980s. An essential ingredient for school improvement among blacks and other minorities, according to Jones-Wilson, is the hiring of professionals who believe that poor children and minority children can learn. New York, Pittsburgh, Milwaukee, and other communities have some schools with histories of lower achievement that now exhibit high achievement. Jones-Wilson claims that there are plenty of "practical action items" available from the National Conference on Educating Black Children and from other sources for educators who want to do the right thing for blacks and other minorities. To achieve these successful outcomes, school systems must "seek to be fair," which is to say that equity in education should not be lost in what Faustine Jones-Wilson calls "the bedlam of the excellence movement."

Charles Flowers, like others who have contributed to this discussion, pinpoints "low teacher expectation" as a major pedagogical problem condemning many black and minority students to an inadequate education. Flowers and other scholars make a case, and make it boldly, that "the quality of teaching" is the main issue. In Flowers' opinion, the school can have a positive effect independent of family circumstances if educators are willing to take risks. While Comer and Haynes would probably support this argument, they add an important codicil: Schools will do what they ought to do when parents of students are involved. In other words, good schooling is a community affair.

Flowers reminds us that the middle school years are critical for minority students, particularly with reference to the development of their capacities to handle mathematics and science. This is a time when racist attitudes can be particularly alienating. To cement relationships between students, parents, and teachers, Flowers and others advocate home visits and school-initiated workshops with parents and community leaders. Such activities, he believes, are particularly appropriate for counselors. These and other suggestions are offered by Flowers in his article "Counsel and Guidance of Black and Other Minority Children in Public Schools."

The 1980s have been a decade of contradictory happenings in education for blacks. While the proportion of blacks graduating from high school increased, the proportion of blacks enrolled in college decreased. Black females outnumbered black males in college; but black males outnumbered black females in doctoral degree graduate programs. Business and management has replaced education as the popular degree among young, college-educated blacks; yet a higher proportion of white-collar blacks are professionals rather than managers. The proportion of black students who need financial aid to go to college has increased during the same period that federal assistance for higher education has decreased. This last coupling explains the smaller proportion of college-going blacks during the 1980s, a decade that harvested the largest proportion of black high school graduates ever. This interesting data were assembled by Antoine Garibaldi in his article on "Blacks in College."

Among the decreasing proportion of black high school graduates who manage to win federally-funded grants, the proprietary "career school" rather than college is the institution of enrollment. In "The Road Taken: Minorities and Proprietary Schools," Robert Rothman tells us that "blacks constitute a disproportionate number of the approximately 1.5 million students in the nearly 6,000 for-profit career schools nationwide." Rothman states that reliable sources have estimated the number of blacks in such schools at one-fifth to one-fourth of all blacks enrolled in post-secondary institutions. These schools offer job-specific training in six months, "a quick return on a student's investment." While some observers see this as a positive outcome, others believe that the education received will not lead to upward mobility, but instead will trap black inner-city young people in a lower socioeconomic status. Indeed, observers told Rothman that some of these schools "at best, [offer] short-term opportunities, and at worse, no help at all."

James Blackwell reports that the contradictory happenings among blacks in education at the college level are also seen at the post-graduate level. As evidence, he offers the findings of a 1987 Robert Wood Johnson Foundation report which indicates that "the admission of black students to medical colleges is declining even though their test scores and other indices of eligibility are improving." Consequently, blacks, who are 11 to 12% of the nation's population, provide less than 4% of the nation's lawyers. Also, they receive less than 4% of the doctorates awarded to U.S. citizens. In his article, "Graduate and Professional Education for Blacks," Blackwell concludes that "our nation's graduate and professional schools are not recruiting, admitting, retaining, and graduating sufficient numbers of blacks." He states that there is a "pool of talent available among black Americans," but that interest in developing it through affirmative action and other efforts by graduate and professional schools seems to have diminished. Because of the increasing proportion of minorities in the population of this nation (estimated to be at one-third two decades into the twenty-first century), we ignore them, ignore their education and the cultivation of their talents, at our peril.

John Williams' article, entitled "System-Wide Title VI Regulation of Higher Education, 1968-1988," confirms Blackwell's contention that our nation has little interest in cultivating through higher education the pool of talent among its minorities. Had there been the political will to do this, Williams said, Title VI provided a legal way. The law required desegregation of public white colleges and universities and enhancement of public black institutions so that they too would attract students of all racial populations. Moreover, the law required that states develop plans to achieve meaningful and timely results. According to Williams, little is known for certain about the outcomes of Title VI. At best, he states, none can claim better than limited results. To date, the federal government has done an inadequate job of data-collection on the implementation of public policy aimed at civil rights goals, particularly with reference to higher education.

Rather than enhancing higher educational opportunities for blacks by using Title VI, Williams states that the federal government seems to have conspired with other institutions to limit such opportunities by reducing federal student aid since 1980. This, in turn, reduced states' capacities to enroll black students in public as well as private colleges and universities. By ignoring or continuing to limit opportunities of minority students who wish to receive a higher education, state governments are following the lead of the federal government.

Williams reports that "no state system over the last twenty years has been found in compliance with Title VI." And he found "no enthusiasm by the federal government to regulate public higher education in the direction of achieving civil rights goals." Consequently, Williams states "[one would be] hard pressed to identify...a single traditionally [public higher education] institution that has a creditable civil rights record of achievement." Although a government of laws, the United States would appear to be reluctant to enforce these laws in behalf of black students wishing to attend white institutions. It is hard to explain the failure of the federal government to enforce a legal requirement of equity. Williams wonders whether such short-sighted, illegal, and in general contra-indicated action is a manifestation of fear that access for blacks to colleges and universities "will compromise the vitality of the American higher education community."

Whenever inequity is unchallenged by high authority and opinion-molders in the nation, discrimination festers and turns ugly. This is precisely what has happened on college and university campuses throughout the United States. Wornie Reed, in an article entitled "The Role of University in Racial Violence on Campus," attributes the violent and insensitive behavior shown by some white students to their black and other minority schoolmates to the "slowdown in racial progress in the 1980s," which he feels was "aided and abetted, if not engineered, by the Reagan administration." Due to the Reagan administration's "war against racial progress" (to use Reed's words), many whites on college and university campuses have misunderstood the reason why affirmative action programs are needed, and they interpret them as acts of discrimination against whites. Without affirmative action, Reed informs us, "it is highly unlikely the discriminatory process will ever end." Reed states that the idea that whites are entitled to privileges that others do not receive is transmitted in the teaching and learning experiences of higher education. And young college students who feel that their privileged position is threatened tend to respond in a violent way.

Willie Pearson, Jr., James Banks, and Meyer Weinberg see the issue raised by Williams–the compromising of the vitality of American higher education–as more of a problem for blacks than for whites. In their opinion, the educational enterprise has compromised, marginalized, and even victimized blacks. The educational enterprise has marginalized blacks by consigning them to selected fields of study and by failing to invite, encourage, and sustain them as worthy participants in science and mathematics. The educational enterprise has compromised blacks by not incorporating ethnic material in the curriculum and by denying the validity of the culture of blacks and other minorities. The educational enterprise has victimized blacks by inadequately cultivating their research skills, underfunding their research proposals, and ignoring the findings of their research reports.

According to Pearson ("Black Participation and Performance in Science, Mathematics and Technical Education"), there is ample evidence of blacks having an interest in science and mathematics. The proportion of blacks who express interest in a field of knowledge that requires quantitative skills is twice as large among those pursuing a bachelor's degree as among those pursuing graduate degrees. We do know that some institutions have been more successful than others in producing black scientists. But the education community has shown no interest in studying such schools to discover why. Also there seems to be no interest in determining why this commitment of blacks to fields of knowledge that require quantitative skills erodes. Pearson has identified "the factors that underlie the career development decisions of blacks" as a research problem that deserves more study.

"The trivialization of ethnic cultures" is a phrase coined by James Banks in his study, "The Social Studies, Ethnic Diversity and Social Change." It is this trivialization that has resulted in our failure to study the career development decisions of blacks and other minorities and the reasons for their varying interests in science, mathematics, business, education, sociology, social work, and other fields. A sound social studies curriculum, according to Banks, should provide "knowledge about why many ethnic groups are victimized by institutional racism and class stratification...." Such knowledge can contribute to genuine equity action by the nation. It would reveal that the fate and future of whites, blacks, and other minorities are intertwined. However, Banks has little hope that this will occur unless there is more effective selection and training of teachers. He calls this "the most challenging and difficult task that lies ahead."

Research has been a traditional way of attaining answers to and understandings of the issues raised in this discussion. Historian Meyer Weinberg informs us that these issues have been "nearly absent from the pages of mainstream...journals." This is so because of "The Politics of Educational Research," the title of Weinberg's article. Weinberg credits the civil rights movement with winning court cases and sponsoring legislation that compelled school authorities to document publicly the general failure to educate poor and minority students. The research that ensued, however, tended to "deflect criticism from the schools" and, according to Weinberg, "placed the responsibility for educational failure upon...[poor, black and minority students] and their families."

Discussions of "racial inequality, racism, and segregation were dealt with only in the pages of publications associated with black scholars and researchers," reports Weinberg. These publications and the issues discussed in them were ignored by the preeminent white scholars and policy makers of the nation. Weinberg found that studies that were "critical of local school districts" were either avoided or ignored. Research universities seldom undertook such studies. Weinberg said the politicalization of education research was so deeply rooted that even civil rights groups and minority-parent organizations hesitated to offer alternative explanations. Their hesitancy probably was due to the fact that research requires technical skills that have been undercultivated among minorities. Thus, their capacity to serve as a countervailing research voice has been severely compromised.

Antoine Garibaldi, in his article "Abating the Shortage of Black Teachers," mentions the declining proportion of black and other minority teachers as a very special problem facing this nation. It is a special cause for concern because the proportion of nonwhite students in major metropolitan school districts is increasing. In some communities the proportion has already exceeded 50%. Garibaldi acknowledges that some blacks are attracted to occupations other than teaching; but he states that other blacks are not going into teaching because they have been pushed out of teacher-training programs, not because they are pulled to more attractive options. He states that some certification requirements use standardized tests that have "eliminated many prospective black teachers and discouraged other potential teacher education majors from choosing that discipline." Clearly the National Teacher Examination (NTE) favors whites over blacks. Between 1978 and 1982, Garibaldi reports, only 18% of Louisiana blacks who took the NTE met the passing score of the state; among whites, 78% passed. Garibaldi, like other scholars mentioned in this discussion, believes that "America's greatest challenge will be to develop effective teacher recruiting strategies." This should involve remedies to improve the certification situation for blacks.

In his study entitled "The Field and Function of Black Studies," James Stewart affirms the observation of W.E.B. Du Bois that we understand the present better by studying the past. The increased number of black students entering predominantly white colleges in the 1960s stimulated the offering of black history as a course of study, and Stewart credits black history with destroying myths about blacks—such as those that portrayed them as passively accepting slavery and subjugation. Black history, according to Stewart, also documented the origins of the self-help movement among blacks and its contribution to their current progress. And finally, black history made available to schools of learning the record of black contributions to the world. Although the program occupies a tenuous position in the curriculum, Black Studies, which includes black history, "has established a beachhead in higher education," according to Stewart, and now needs to be integrated into the K-12 curriculum. Moreover, this domain of inquiry should be extended from the humanities, the social, and the behavioral sciences to the natural and physical sciences. Ultimately, Black Studies, if pursued in a comprehensive way as recommended by Stewart, should contribute to theories of history and social change. Stewart's comprehensive conception of Black Studies would prove beneficial to all learners.

Summary and Interpretation

Following the celebration of the bicentennial year, the upward trend in the proportion of blacks enrolled in colleges and universities turned downward. The upward turn of the 1960s and early 1970s could be interpreted as fulfillment of the constitutional requirement of equal protection of the laws for all, while the downward turn in the 1980s suggests a lack of national commitment to the higher education of African-Americans. Blacks had hope during the late 1950s and the 1960s, but despair thereafter, as local education agencies desegregated more whites than blacks and gave whites greater access to magnet schools and other improvements.

This review suggests that, even during periods of progress in the attainment of racial justice, the forces against such justice are ever present. Recognition of the coexistence of yin and yang, good and evil, within any community, including the nation-state, should protect against undue optimism in times of success and undue pessimism in times of failure. The seeds of racial retrogression in educational opportunities were latent during the season of racial progress; likewise, the experience of commitment to racial justice is not absent but in remission as we witness a national mood that accepts and sanctions inequity.

We learn from this analysis that racial progress in education is not inevitable, nor is it continuous. A period of arrested racial justice in education need not become permanent. The progress towards equality depends on the action or inaction of people in power and people out of power.

This nation consists of several population groups–racial, ethnic, and other–that interact and influence each other through the mediums of power that each commands. The groups that are classified as dominant have greater power potential than others. The groups that are classified as subdominant have less power potential than others. Power is the capacity to influence or force others to behave in a prescribed way.

Numbers, organization, and resources are power attributes. In the United States, whites are the majority; they have operational control over most organizations and institutions and access to many of the resources that are valued in this nation. Whites, therefore, may be classified as the dominant people of power among racial populations. It should be stated, however, that a population group dominant in one sector of society may not be dominant in all sectors. Also, a dominant group may not be dominant always. Likewise, a group subdominant in one sector of society could be dominant in another. Among population groups in the United States, blacks in most sectors are subdominant. But they may not be subdominant always or in all sectors of society.

Subdominant groups have less capacity to influence or force others to behave in a prescribed way. No groups, including those that are subdominant, are without any power. Subdominants as well as dominants have veto power. They can disrupt orderly ways of doing things. Because disruption is invoked usually to express discontent, it is a method more frequently used by subdominants. Subdominants, however, are reluctant to use their veto power because they, as well as dominants, could experience harm as a result of disruption.

When dominants act in ways that harm subdominants and refuse to change their harmful policies and practices, subdominants have alternatives: they may submit or resist. Neither action guarantees relief from oppression. An intransigent dominant group is not likely to change conventional ways of doing things unless challenged to do so by subdominants. Subdominants who are reluctant to challenge unjust customs are likely to continue to experience oppression for a long period of time.

As we review the happenings in education in this nation since the 1940s, we see that substantial improvements that benefited blacks and other minorities resulted only after they challenged the establishment, the dominant people of power, to behave differently. The legal challenges of segregated education by blacks under the leadership of the National Association for the Advancement of Colored People (NAACP) and other civil rights groups resulted in the 1954 and 1955 Brown I and II decisions by the Supreme Court. These decisions declared segregated education inherently unequal, and therefore illegal. Since our nation did not make a timely response to requirements of the Court, blacks increased their pressure on the establishment to do the right thing through a series of veto-action episodes. This pressure was provided by Martin Luther King, Jr., the Southern Christian Leadership Conference, the Congress of Racial Equality, the Student Nonviolent Coordinating Committee, and other individuals and groups. The pressure was stepped up through disruptive demonstrations and marches, a new category of response called "nonviolent direct action." Such challenges resulted in the Civil Rights Act of 1964 and the Voting Rights Act of 1965.

The Civil Rights Act contained titles that prohibited racial discrimination in publicly-supported education and in other sectors of society. To enhance representative government and to achieve more diversity in official policy-making bodies were goals of the Voting Rights Act. Eventually, this act would affect the racial and ethnic composition of elected school boards. White-dominated governmental structures at local, state, and federal levels demurred in fully implementing the changes required by these laws. But, after the death of Martin Luther King, Jr., and the unrelenting veto actions set loose by this tragic event, the nation began to make an appropriate response to challenges by blacks for change, particularly in the area of education. Thus, the middle years of the 1970s marked the apex of racial desegregation in elementary and secondary schools and in institutions of higher learning in the United States. In the light of retrogressive activity during the 1980s, one could conclude that the sacrificial death of Martin Luther King, Jr., in 1968 influenced the conscience of the dominant people of power in this country for nearly a decade.

Obviously, new challenges by blacks are needed to sustain and maintain the equity in education that was begun. One can understand how the energies of one generation of blacks to mount new challenges have been spent and exhausted. It is not yet clear what kinds of challenges will be brought forth by future generations of blacks. But one fact is certain: Challenge will be necessary in a nation that is unresponsive to the desire of subdominant people to be free and to participate as responsible decision makers in the community. Through challenge, subdominants cease cooperating in their own oppression and become courageous resisters of injustice. In the United States, as in other human societies, injustice for anyone ultimately is injustice for everyone. Thus, subordinants who resist injustice act in behalf of the whole society.

We also have learned from this review and analysis that challenge, while necessary and essential, need not be disruptive if dominant people of power make an appropriate response. An appropriate and effective response for dominants is to pursue justice with compassion. For justice cannot coexist with injustice; that fairness which is not universal and impartial is not in the end fairness at all. Compassionate people offer more than they are required to give and take less than they are entitled to receive. When dominant people of power follow this course of action, there may still be a need for subdominants to challenge, but no need for them to disrupt, since a compassionate response will be timely.

Whites, in general, have not responded with generosity or magnanimity to three decades of challenge by blacks that this nation live up to its creed of justice and equality for all in education. They did not do what they ought to have done, and they did many things that they ought not to have done. Because there was no justice, we reaped a whirlwind of social discord in the 1950s and in the 1960s. During the first half of the 1970s, whites began to make a compassionate response to the courageous challenges of blacks. At long last the challenge and response processes were synchronized and in harmony. Consequently, disorder diminished and disruption through "direct action" disappeared; change was orderly and continuous. The gap between the races decreased in various measures of educational progress.

As stability and peace returned to our cities and disruptive challenges faded into history, the dominant forces began to backslide and ceased to respond with compassion. They forget how stability and peace had been won, became less generous and magnanimous, became self-centered and arrogant. Practices of oppression returned during the 1980s. Whites blamed black victims for failures in their home life and in their schooling. Our nation suffers from loss of recent memory. It has forgotten how it coped with strife one generation ago, how courage and compassion helped to overcome our division and unite our people in trust. These synchronized processes were something of great value. They are necessary and essential today.

This essay challenges the nation to rediscover that courage and compassion in education and in other sectors of our society. This is the major lesson that we have learned from this review and analysis: Failure to courageously challenge injustice is folly; failure to make a compassionate response is folly. Thus, dominant and subdominant people have a joint responsibility to reform the educational enterprise. Subdominants have the responsibility of initiating proposals to redress reform. Dominants have the responsibility of refining such proposals and integrating them into the laws and practices of the society.

The Supreme Court in the Brown II decision of 1955 committed the error of assigning "the primary responsibility" for fashioning desegregation plans for segregated public school systems to "school authorities." The Court did not require school authorities, the dominant people of power, to consult with or otherwise enlist the help of the plaintiff class, the subdominant people of power, in the development of remedial plans. Again ignoring the principle of joint responsibility, the Court also incorrectly assigned the initiation of redress and reform that is uniquely a property of subdominants to the dominant people of power. It was inappropriate to ask the same people who established, maintained, and operated segregated schools to devise a plan to disestablish them. They were not the appropriate power group to initiate reform.

We assert that initiation of redress or reform proposals should be a prerogative of subdominants. Reforms that are designed to fulfill the needs and interests of the least among us are likely to fulfill the needs and interests of the society as a whole. But reforms that are designed for the brightest and best learners may be of little, if any, help for the handicapped, for the oppressed, for the slow learner. Traditionally, the dominant people of power have focused on outcome measures as the criteria of successful education. Subdominant people of power tend to focus on input and process experiences as the essentials of effective education. Since input, along with process and outcome experiences, all contribute to education, the focus of both dominants and subdominants is necessary in the achievement of reform.

Conclusions and Recommendations

Gunnar Myrdal found that segregation in public schools was a means of perpetuating economic discrimination against blacks. Using the Fourteenth Amendment as the constitutional base, the NAACP won several court cases which demonstrated that blacks did not receive equal protection of the law because their segregated and inadequately financed schools did not provide an education equal in quality to that received by whites. The Supreme Court found in *Brown v. Board of Education* that segregated education is inherently unequal. The ruling of the court seemed to sustain the finding by Myrdal. On the basis of evidence reviewed and analyzed, the nation is obligated to eliminate all forms of segregated education. This is the lawful way to redress the grievances brought by blacks in that landmark court case.

In the process of implementing school desegregation law, confusion and contradiction appeared. White-dominated school boards that opposed integrated education designed desegregation plans that produced more desegregation of whites than of blacks. Whites also urged courts to declare school systems unitary even though more whites than blacks experienced desegregation and some blacks remained in segregated schools. Some blacks, according to the review and analysis, point to the achievement outcomes of effective schools following the Comer model as evidence that racial separation is not always detrimental to the education of blacks. However, they acknowledge that a white-dominated governmental system that initiated segregation in the past for the purpose of discriminating against subdominant people is unlikely to appropriate sufficient funds to make racially segregated black schools effective.

We conclude that the full benefits of school desegregation have been experienced less often by blacks because of the confused and contra-indicated way in which the law has been implemented.

- The Court did not provide criteria for determining the educational effectiveness of desegregation.

- The Court did not provide any definition of a unitary public school system.

- The Court did not indicate how promptly a segregated school system should be desegregated.

- The methods of achieving desegregation evolved over a decade-and-a-half in a haphazard and piecemeal fashion.

- The Court did not identify sources of technical assistance for the development of school desegregation plans.

- The Court did not always cite the state as a co-conspirator in desegregation cases, although the state is the ultimate educational authority.

- The Court seldom found that segregated schooling was harmful to whites as well as to blacks and other minorities.

Contra-indicated in the Court order granting relief were these prescriptions:

- Local educational agencies that operated segregated schools were delegated the responsibility of planning and implementing a unitary system of desegregated schools.

- Local educational agencies were instructed to proceed in good faith and with deliberate speed but were not required to desegregate schools promptly.

- Local educational agencies were permitted to delay the implementation of desegregation plans if in the public interest (as opposed to the interest of the plaintiff class) more time was needed.

- Local educational agencies were required to implement a plan that provided immediate relief to segregated schools but were not required to demonstrate how continuing relief under changing demographic conditions would be maintained.

- Local educational agencies were not required to diversify the membership of school boards so that the participation of majority and minority parents in educational public policy is guaranteed.

To overcome these deficiencies, we recommend the following:

- State government should be held accountable by the Court as the responsible public authority that will guarantee equal access to public schools and therefore will be required to help finance desegregation and monitor its implementation.

- Definitions of unitary school systems should be promulgated that do not accommodate any segregated schools and that recognize desegregation as valid and achievable regardless of whether blacks and other racial populations or whites are the majority in a local school system.

- The Court should adhere to the dictum that justice delayed is justice denied and require all segregated school systems to desegregate promptly and to implement plans that will grant continuous desegregative relief under conditions of changing demography.

- State or federal law should require that local school authorities be elected by single-member districts rather than at-large to guarantee diversity in the decision-making structure, and if appointed that persons of dissimilar racial and ethnic backgrounds be chosen.

A majority of blacks prefer a desegregated education for their children and a majority of whites will send their children to racially balanced schools. Most reform plans have provided desegregated experiences for whites more often than for blacks. We conclude that school desegregation has been the engine for social reform in this nation, that it has been relatively successful in all sections of the nation, but that it has been less beneficial for blacks because they have been excluded by school authorities from the process of reform and because they have disproportionately experienced the burden of transportation to accomplish systemic desegregation.

To overcome such unfairness, we recommend that

- The rights of blacks who won the school desegregation Court cases should be protected and not compromised, and that their grievances should be lawfully redressed regardless of the attitudes of whites about the requirements of the Constitution to grant equal protection of the laws.

- Desegregation of all school systems should proceed promptly and all population groups should have proportional access to all schools in accordance with their representation in the local school district, even in school systems in which whites are a minority. This principle should apply to all programs, including magnet schools, gifted and talented programs, and special education programs.

- Better methods of desegregation planning are needed, involving multiracial teams of planners that do not hold student assignments hostage to segregated neighborhood zones that contributed to the original crisis of segregated schools.

Finally, we recommend that

- The common school should fulfill its mission to majority and minority students by relating to each student group in a population-specific way.

- All school authorities should be taught that all students can learn, that none is unworthy of receiving a quality education, and that such education is likely to be offered for minority members of society in settings of sympathetic understanding that consider the whole student, including his or her particular learning style and cultural uniqueness.

- Blockages in entry to a variety of higher education opportunities should be eliminated for blacks by providing more admissions requirements such as standardized tests that are not related to school performance and job success.

- The federal government must provide more assistance to black students. In historically black institutions, more than 80% of the students have large loans. Grants, not loans, should be available to these students.

- Since historically black colleges and universities have always accepted the majority of the so-called "disadvantaged" and "underprepared" cohort of black students, more institutional aid should be provided them. This will enable these institutions to expand their academic programs so that needy black students can have the chance to obtain a college degree, to be prepared for a professional opportunity in law, medicine, or graduate education.

- More recruitment of black teachers is needed to guarantee that our youth will be taught by teachers who have knowledge of and respect for ethnic history and diversity.

- More black students must be directed toward careers in science and mathematics by providing them with more exposure to these fields at secondary school levels and by sustaining their interests in these fields through graduate study.

- Specific strategies should be employed to promote more research on racial and ethnic issues in education.

- Research and evaluation studies of a school reform should be conducted by racially diversified research staffs so that the academic progress of students is studied in a comparative way. Such researchers are likely to investigate the experiences as unique to each population group, not likely to analyze the experiences of any group as deviant and outside the mainstream.

- Foundations, religious organizations, and other voluntary associations should provide resources and other assistance to blacks for community organization and community development that will enable subdominants to effectively challenge dominants to make effective responses in the areas of educational reform.

These recommendations, if adopted and diligently pursued by the nation, should enhance the educational reform process so that excellence may be pursued without compromising equity. Moreover, the fulfillment of these recommendations will indicate that fairness is the central criterion against which the efficacy of all educational reform should be assessed.

6

African-Americans and the Administration of Justice

E. Yvonne Moss

The status of African-Americans in relationship to the administration of justice has improved since the 1940s. Significantly, however, researchers continue to find racial discrimination and racial disadvantage operating in various aspects of the criminal justice process in numerous jurisdictions. Such findings are unacceptable in a society that claims to honor equal justice under law.

Historically, the law, the police, the courts, and the prisons have been used as instruments of oppression and subordination based on race. When the Supreme Court in its *Brown* decision (1954) articulated for the first time in constitutional history that black Americans had a right to equal protection of the law, it began the process of repudiating those historically oppressive instruments and began the process of reconciling black Americans to the institutions of criminal justice. The *Furman* decision (1972) which outlawed the arbitrary and discriminatory use of the death penalty and the *Coker* decision (1977) which outlawed the use of the death penalty in rape cases (over 90% of those executed for this crime were black men) were moves in the right direction, but discrimination and disadvantage based on race continued to be found in this and other important aspects of criminal justice processing.

If the nation is to complete the process of reconciliation in this area, if it is to win the trust of black Americans in its police, courts, and correctional policies, it must move to eliminate all vestiges of racial bias from the administration of justice. To aid in that process, scholars composing the study group on the administration of justice have closely examined the existing literature, made assessments of contemporary practices, and produced an evaluation of criminal justice that identifies those areas where discrimination abounds.

One of the areas of concern is the unequal application of the death penalty. Between 1930 and 1967, 3,586 people were executed. Over half of those executed for murder and 92% of those executed for rape, were black Americans. Some scholars attribute the 1972 *Furman* decision in part to this overwhelmingly disproportionate use of capital punishment. The informal moratorium on executions which began in 1967 continued for another five years after the *Furman* decision abolished the death penalty as it was being imposed, because of its arbitrary and discriminatory application. That moratorium ended in 1977 after the Supreme Court ruled in *Gregg* (1976) and four companion cases that capital punishment was constitutional under certain circumstances.

In the decade between 1977 and 1987, black Americans continued to represent a higher proportion of those executed than the proportion of black citizens in the population. Of the 70 persons put to death during those years, 24 were black Americans (34.3%), 42 were white Americans (60%), and 4 were Hispanic (5.7%). Of the 1,901 persons on death row in 1987, 50.4% were white Americans, 41.4% were African-Americans, 5.8% were Hispanics, and 1.4% were Native Americans. In spite of all the efforts to make the death penalty statutes more fair during the last fifteen years, the minority population on death row had been reduced by less than 1%.

In capital punishment cases the variable exerting the strongest predictive power in correlation with sentencing is the *race of the victim*. After controlling for 230 variables, a massive statistical study done in the *McCleskey* case (1987) demonstrated that defendants charged with killing whites are 4.3 times as likely to receive the death penalty as defendants charged with killing blacks. Black defendants charged with killing whites are sentenced to death seven times more often than whites who kill blacks. Studies on the use of the death penalty since *Gregg* indicate that racial disparities in capital sentencing remain. Black defendants convicted of killing whites are more likely to receive the death penalty than any others convicted of capital crimes.

In *McCleskey v. Kemp* (1987) the Supreme Court considered a petition to overturn a death penalty conviction in Georgia. The petition was supported by a massive statistical study using sophisticated statistical analysis. The study demonstrated that in Georgia the race of the defendant and the race of the victim were critical variables in the decision to execute. The court in its ruling acknowledged that disparity was proven in the imposition of the death penalty. The justices further acknowledged that this disparity reflected racial bias against black defendants. Nevertheless the court in a 5-4 decision ruled:

> . . . [S]uch discrepancies do not violate the Equal Protection Clause of the Fourteenth Amendment. In order to prevail under that Clause, a criminal defendant (unlike an employment discrimination plaintiff, for example) must prove that decisionmakers in this case acted with discriminatory purpose. (*McCleskey v. Kemp*, 1987)

Reminiscent of *Plessy's* 1896 legal justification of segregation, the *McCleskey* ruling provides a legal justification for the discriminatory application of the death penalty. Execution is the most extreme form of punishment our nation imposes on its citizens. Giving legal sanction to discrimination in the application of the death sentence makes a mockery of the ideal of equal justice under law, and it moves the country backwards to the pre-1967 era when capital punishment was systematic manifestation of racial oppression.

Research on sentencing in categories other than capital punishment indicate that racial discrimination varies widely across the United States. Despite disagreements over the reasons and the significance of the findings, researchers agree that black criminal defendants receive more severe sentences than do white defendants. While there should be concern that studies of disparity in sentencing have arrived at different conclusions on the issue of racial bias, such an outcome is expected, given the highly decentralized and localized structure of the American judiciary with regard to criminal matters. It should come as no surprise that blacks are discriminated against in some jurisdictions but not in others. Most discrimination is found in the South, but not exclusively so. Aggregate studies do not separate men and women in evaluating outcomes, and this distorts the findings because female defendants are treated less severely by the courts than are males. Still, reputable studies like the *Michigan Felony Sentencing Project* (Zalman et al, 1979) and the *Minnesota Sentencing Guidelines Commission Study* (1982) continue to provide evidence that race is a consistent factor in criminal sentencing. These studies have been used to fashion new judicial policy nationally as well as in other states.

A number of conclusions are evident. Blacks males are more likely than white males to be sentenced to prison. Whites receive the probation option more often than blacks in similar circumstances. The race of the victim is important to understanding how discrimination gets involved in sentencing. And there tends to be more discrimination in the less formal aspects of the adjudication procedures, including plea-bargaining, than in the more formal and open trial process. This last observation is especially noteworthy because over 90% of all cases in most jurisdictions *do not go to trial*. Plea-bargaining is the process by which most criminal cases are disposed of. That most discrimination is found in these less formal aspects of criminal justice processing should be the cause of considerable concern. Most of the work in the administration of justice is done in the less formal, invisible adjudication processes, away from public scrutiny.

Research on discrimination has focused primarily on sentencing, but it now seems clear that race is a significant factor in previous stages of the process. These stages include police treatment of suspects and arrests, prosecutors' decisions to file or dismiss cases, and pretrial treatment of defendants, including bail procedures. One study of a Houston court found that prosecutors consistently failed to charge whites with capital crimes against blacks even with strong evidence. The reason given was that juries simply would not convict a white person of a capital offense against a black person. Rather than lose the conviction entirely, prosecutors would charge white defendants who had committed capital crimes against black persons with a lesser offense. Thus racial bias as a factor in the final disposition of a criminal case may be incorporated into a decision calculus at various stages of the process. The consequence is the same. Contrary to legal theory, ideals about judicial process, and common standards of decency and fairness, race oftentimes is a primary factor in criminal processing.

Researchers such as Kleck (1981) and Wilbanks (1987) reject the hypothesis that widespread and pervasive discrimination exists against black people in sentencing. Their claims are questionable at best. Wilbanks uses *implication* and *speculation* rather than empirical data to question the findings of racial effects. Kleck uses an arbitrary classification scheme to exclude from his analysis studies that found racial bias in less than half of the offenses studied. Such intellectual sleights of hand should not be used as an excuse by policy makers to ignore this vital issue. Racial discrimination will not be found in every state or every locality in the United States. Yet scholarly studies continue to support the finding of racial bias and disadvantage in various jurisdictions throughout the country. When evidence of racial disadvantage and discrimination is uncovered, policy makers in criminal justice have a responsibility to eradicate such bias. One of those areas is juvenile justice.

Minority youth are incarcerated at rates three to four times higher than white youth. The data on the heavy involvement of minority youth in violent crime cannot, by itself, explain such high rates of incarceration. Minority incarceration in public correctional facilities *increased* 26% to 5,035, between 1977 and 1982. Black youngsters accounted for almost two-thirds of this increase. Concomitantly, the number of white youth in public facilities *decreased* by 7%. Earlier policies to remove minor offenders from confinement mostly benefited white youth. In 1982 incarceration rates per 100,000 by race and gender were: 810 (black males); 183 (white males); 481 (Hispanic males); 98 (black females); 38 (white females); and 40 (Hispanic females).

The rates of minority incarceration continue to grow at a faster rate than the confinement of white youth. The data on minority youth crime are ambiguous and contradictory, and thus do not explain the higher incarceration rates for minority youth. The overrepresentation of minorities in arrest statistics is not as large as the disproportionate number of minority youth who are incarcerated. Additionally, the arrest statistics may overestimate the extent of minority involvement in serious youth crime because black youth are more likely to be arrested and charged with more serious crimes than whites engaged in the same activities. The discrepancies between arrest statistics and incarceration rates have led to concerns about discrimination within the adjudication phase of criminal processing for juveniles.

Our evaluation of juvenile courts indicates that minority and poor juveniles have been subjected to widespread, systematic discrimination. Earlier research efforts that focused on the final disposition of the case, or on one decision point, ignored important discriminatory factors. The influence of class, race, or gender may be most evident in initial stages of the juvenile court process (detention decision or screening decision); but as a juvenile becomes increasingly enmeshed in the judicial system, the impact of social characteristics is incorporated into the newly defined process variables, decision outcomes that inform subsequent decisions. Bias is incorporated into initial legal decisions, and final disposition, the most commonly examined decision, is the last juncture and the point at which this transformation is most likely to be complete.

When juvenile court decision making is studied as a multiphased process, the following conclusions are evident. Black youths receive more severe dispositions than white youths. Black youths are much more likely to be detained prior to a hearing, and somewhat more likely to be handled formally. As with adults, this is significant since those detained as well as those handled formally receive more severe dispositions. Consequently, early juvenile court decisions predispose black youths to more severe final dispositions. One way racial bias operates in juvenile courts is when social characteristics like race get transformed into legal variables, and both sets of factors act independently and together to affect the treatment of black youths in the juvenile justice system.

When the situation of black Americans in correctional institutions is reviewed, what is immediately evident is that the numbers of black Americans incarcerated in the country's prisons are immensely disproportionate to their percentage in the general U.S. population. Black Americans, together with smaller percentages of Hispanics, Puerto Ricans , and members of other racial minorities, currently constitute the majority of Americans prisoners (Jacobs, 1979). In 1982, black Americans accounted for approximately 12% of the U.S. population and 48% of the prison population (Bureau of Justice Statistics, 1982). Black prisoners under the sentence of death for capital offenses represent almost one-half of all persons awaiting execution (Bureau of Justice Statistics, 1981). Perhaps most alarming of all, black offenders represent the highest percentages in prison populations in those states where the percentage of black citizens in the general population is low (Institute for Public Policy and Management, 1986).

Although there are arguments over why such gross disparities occur, the facts of disproportionality are indisputable. The capacity of our analytic tools may not be sufficient to discern the reasons. Yet we know what we need to know to cite the administration of justice and corrections as a high priority for effective policy formulation. Sensible policy making requires an acknowledgement of *both* the propensity of some individuals to commit crime *and* the capacity of society to encourage and abet criminality. Sober policies and programs are needed that address both the individual and the societal dimensions of the problem with equity and fairness.

The development of policy options needed to eradicate racial bias in corrections, like those needed in other criminal justice institutions, requires not only a concern for eliminating discrimination but also a desire to improve the substantive performance of these institutions in accomplishing the lofty ideals of their mission. In corrections the policy choices for most communities are simple: to continue to spend large sums of money to build prisons and maintain corrections as a growth industry or to spend roughly equal amounts of money to keep 40 to 60% of the incarcerated population out of prison and engaged in socially productive lives. Criticisms of racial bias made against the criminal justice process are taken by some as evidence that black Americans are "soft on crime." On the contrary, studies of black attitudes on crime and the police reveal that black citizens want fair, effective, "tough" law enforcement. What they do not want is to be presumed to be criminal simply because they are black. When considering the status of black Americans and the administration of justice, the primary question is not whether a uniform indictment or a clean bill of health can be given to American justice with regard to racial discrimination. The important question is whether racial (or gender or status) discrimination is acceptable in any jurisdiction, in any aspect of the judicial process.

Amid national concern over drugs and violent crime, the issue of racial bias in criminal proceedings may not be considered a priority. However, the respect for law necessary to reduce our crime problems is not possible if punishment is perceived to be skewed by race. The system loses legitimacy if citizens are punished or not punished because of their color or the color of their victims, or because of their education and income. Racial disadvantage and discrimination are unacceptable in any system of justice that strives both symbolically and substantively for fair and impartial treatment of those accused and fair and effect punishment of those found guilty.

Policy Issues

A wide range of policy options are available to address problems of bias when uncovered. These include:

- Increased employment of black persons at *all* levels of the criminal justice system.

- Bail reform—when bail systems are used as preventive detention for the poor rather than to ensure appearance at trial;

- Upgrading the quality of defense counsel available to indigents with measures such as greater privatization of indigent defense, higher pay, and better working conditions of public defender roles, which might include restructuring the job;

- Establishment of prosecution standards along with guidelines by which prosecutors are held accountable, where there is indication of the abuse of prosecutorial discretion;

- Cultural sensitivity training for criminal justice personnel, including judges;

- Guidelines on judicial conduct with respect to discriminatory treatment added to those developed and monitored by judicial conduct commissions;

- Judicial recruitment that stimulates diversity on the bench;

- Better training for judges and other criminal justice personnel;

- Changes in legal education and professional practices that encourage the development of discriminatory attitudes and values;

- Legal scholarship that challenges aspects of the legal tradition that encourage racism.

References

Brown v. Board of Education, Topeka, Kansas 347 U.S. 483; 98L. Ed. 873; 74 S. Ct. 686 (1954).

Bureau of Justice Statistics. (1981). Death-Row Prisoners, 1981. In *Bulletin*. Washington, D.C.: U.S. Government Printing Office.

Bureau of Justice (1982). *Statistics*. Washington, D.C.: U.S. Government PrintingOffice.

Coker v. Georgia, 433 U.S. 485 (1977).

Dannefer, D. & Schutt, R.K. (1982). Race and Juvenile Processing in Court andPolice Agencies. *America Journal Sociology, 87*, 1113-32.

Furman v. Georgia, 408 U.S. 238 (1972).

Gregg v. Georgia, 96 S. Ct. 2950 (1976).

Institute for Public Policy and Management. (1986). *Racial and Ethnic Disparities in Imprisonment*. Seattle: University of Washington.

Jacobs, B. (1979). Race Relations and the Prisoner Subculture. In N. Morris & M. Tonry (Eds.), *Crime and Justice: An Annual Review of Research*. Chicago: University of Chicago Press.

Kleck, G. (1981). Racial Discrimination in Sentencing: A Critical Evaluation of the Evidence with Additional Evidence on the Death Penalty. American *Sociological Review, 6*, 783-805.

McCleskey v. Kemp, 481 U.S. 279 (1987); also see 107 S. Ct. 1756 (1987).

Minnesota Sentencing Guidelines. (1982). *Preliminary Report on the Development and Impact of the Minnesota Guidelines*. St. Paul: Minnesota Guidelines Commission.

Plessy v. Ferguson, 163 U.S. 537 (1896).

Wilbanks, W. (1987). *The Myth of a Racist Criminal Justice System*. Monterey, CA: Brooks/Cole.

Zalman, M., Ostrom, C.W., Jr., Guilliams, P., & Peaslee, G. (1979). *Sentencing in Michigan: Report of the Michigan Felony Sentencing Project*. Lansing, MI: State Court Administrative Office.

7

Health and Medical Care

Wornie L. Reed and Carolyne W. Arnold

Racial disadvantage in the United States–especially that of blacks in relation to whites–is nowhere more telling than in mortality rates and life expectancy. Blacks do not live as long as whites. They suffer disadvantages in health status and in access to medical services. The National Center for Health Statistics reported that in 1986 life expectancy for blacks declined for the second year in a row–the first back-to-back annual decline in this century. The black rate declined to 69.4 years while the white rate increased to a record high of 75.4 years.

Health Status

Blacks are at greater risk than whites for both morbidity and mortality. That is to say that they are in poorer health than whites and die earlier. Blacks are at higher risk of death throughout the life span, except at very advanced ages. One means of expressing these racial differentials in mortality is the "excess deaths" index. This index expresses the difference between the number of actual deaths among blacks and the number of deaths that would have occurred if blacks had experienced the same death rates for each age and sex as the white population. During the period 1979 to 1981, for black males and females combined, excess deaths represented 47% of the total annual deaths in blacks 45 years old or less, and 42% in blacks aged 70 years or less.

Another measure used to illustrate racial differentials in mortality is "person-years of life lost," which incorporates the impact of the age of death on black/white differences. Results indicate that among black men, over 900,000 years of life before age 70 are lost each year in excess of the person-years lost by white men. Among black females nearly 600,000 person-years are lost annually in excess of the loss among white females. If blacks had the same death rates as whites, 59,000 black deaths a year would not occur.

Mortality Rates

There has been a widening of the gap in mortality rates between blacks and whites. For example, in 1950 the adjusted death rates per 100,000 residents for all causes was 841.5, and in 1980 it was 585.8, a 30.4% decrease for the overall population. In 1950 the rate for black males was 1,373 per 100,000 black residents and for white males it was 963.1, a difference of 410 per 100,000 persons. The differential deficit ratio (the extent to which the black rate exceeds the white rate) was 42.6%. In 1980 the death rate for black males was 1,112.8 per 100,000 persons and for white males 745.3 per 100,000, a difference of 367.5. Even though the difference had decreased, the differential deficit ratio of deaths from all causes between black males and white males had increased from 42.6% to 49.3%. This was an increase of 6.7% deficit over the 30-year period.

Among females, however, the differential deficit ratio decreased between 1950 and 1980. For black females the death rate for all causes in 1950 was 1,106 per 100,000. For white females it was 650 per 100,000, a difference of 456.7 and a differential deficit ratio of 70.3%. By 1980 this gap had decreased to 56.3%, a decrease of 17.1%.

Infant Mortality

The infant mortality rate is one of the most critical indices used nationally and internationally to interpret the status of a population group. The national infant mortality rate in the United States has been steadily decreasing; between 1970 and 1985 the rate was cut in half. In fact, it is reasonably close to the 1% rate that was established as a policy objective for the 1980s.

The black infant mortality rate is nearly twice the white rate. While the white rate in 1985 was 9.3 deaths per 1,000 live births, the black rate was 18.2 deaths per 1,000 live births. Another way of stating this is that some 6,000 black infants who die each year would be living if the infant mortality rate for black infants was as low as that for white infants.

Although both white and black infant mortality rates have decreased substantially over the period between 1950 and 1985, the gap between black and white rates increased. In 1950 the black infant mortality rate exceeded the white rate by less than two thirds; in 1985 the black rate exceeded the white rate by almost 100%. One of the primary factors related to infant mortality is socioeconomic status; there is also a race effect over and above the class effect.

Selected Diseases

In addition to higher "all cause mortality rates," blacks experience disproportionately more severe mortality rates than whites for a number of diseases or conditions. Ranked number one, of course, is infant mortality. Following infant mortality are heart disease, cancer, and strokes, in that order. Other major health problems are lead poisoning, AIDS, and homicide.

Heart Disease and Stroke

Heart disease and stroke cause more deaths and disabilities in the United States than any other disease. Together they represent nearly 40% of all excess deaths for blacks less than 70 years of age.

Disease of the Heart

In 1950 total deaths due to diseases of the heart was 307.6 per 100,000 persons. By 1983 this had decreased to 188.8 per 100,000 population, a 38.6 % decrease. For black males deaths due to heart disease was 415.5 per 100,000 and for whites males 381.1, for a difference of 34.4 and a differential deficit ratio of 9.0%. By 1983 the rate for blacks was 308.2 per 100,000 and for whites 257.8 per 100,000, for a difference of 50.4 and a differential deficit ratio of 20.0, an increase in the deficit of 122.2%.

For black females the death rate in 1950 was 349.5 per 100,000 persons and for white females 223.6 per 100,000, for a difference of 125.9 per 100,000 and a differential deficit ratio of 56.4. By 1983 the differential deficit ratio between black females and white females had decreased only slightly to 51.1%.

Cerebrovascular Diseases

Total deaths due to cerebrovascular diseases in 1950 was 88.8 per 100,000 persons. In 1983 the rate was 34.4 per 100,000, a 61.3% decrease. In 1950 the rate for black males was 146.2 per 100,000 and for white males 87.0 per 100,000, for a difference of 59.2 and a differential deficit ratio of 68.0%. By 1980 the differential deficit ratio had *increased* to 82.4%.

The death rate was 155.6 per 100,000 persons in 1950 for black females and 79.7 per 100,000 for white females, a difference of 75.9 and a differential deficit ratio of 95.2%. By 1983 the difference had decreased from 75.9% to 24.2%, a percentage decrease of 68.1%. However, the differential deficit ratio was 81.8%, a decrease of only 14.1% over the 30-year period.

As a result of conceptual and methodological problems there are continuing disagreements about the prevalence of coronary heart disease (CHD). Available data suggest that black women have excess prevalence of CHD in comparison to white women, and black men have equal or greater prevalence rates in comparison to whites until age 64. After age 64 the rate for white men exceeds that of black men. Thus, black men have an equal prevalence rate and a higher mortality rate from coronary heart disease. These data suggest that blacks do not receive appropriate medical care.

Cancer

Cancer is second only to heart disease as the most frequent cause of death in the United States. During the 1950s and 1960s cancer deaths were increasing twice as fast in the black population as in the white population. Black females are slightly less likely to have cancer than white females, but black males are significantly more likely to have cancer than white males. Although black females are less likely to have cancer than white females, they are more than 20% less likely to survive cancer. And black males are nearly 30% less likely than white males to survive cancer.

Over the past 30 years white predominance has been replaced by black predominance in both incidence and mortality rates among males and black predominance in female mortality from cancer. Many cancers are related to such risk factors as tobacco, tobacco and alcohol combined, occupation, dietary patterns, and nutritional status. Such risk factors have been shown to account for approximately 72% of cancer mortality and 69% of incidence.

When adjustments are made for stage at diagnosis in cancer patient survival studies, survival differences decrease between blacks and whites, and when adjustments for socioeconomic status (SES) are made, the disparities between the two groups are further reduced. Additional factors that may contribute to poor cancer survival in blacks include delay in detection and treatment differences. For all stages of diagnosis, blacks have lower survival rates than whites; however, these differences tend to decrease across individual stage categories for a number of cancer sites. This is due to the greater distribution of lower stages (less advanced cancer) in white patients, which means that blacks have later diagnoses, suggesting delay in detection and treatment.

SES may be related to cancer survival rates through two factors related to health services behavior—medical care and cancer-related knowledge. SES is a factor in the source of medical care, a point that suggests differentials in the quality, appropriateness, and technical sophistication of medical care received. For example, blacks tend to have episodic treatment at hospital clinics rather than continuing treatment by a single physician. A study of black and white cancer patients at a VA hospital showed that there was no difference (except for bladder cancer) in survival between the two groups; in this instance because they received the same type of cancer care.

Data on blacks' cancer-related knowledge, attitudes, and practices are limited. However, the limited data suggests that blacks tend to know less about cancer than whites, that blacks underestimate the prevalence of cancer, and that blacks have less knowledge about cancer warning signs. In addition, blacks have been reported to be more pessimistic than whites about their chances for survival. They tend to be more fatalistic and are less likely to believe that early detection makes a difference and that existing treatments are effective. So it is not surprising that blacks are less likely than whites to see a physician in response to symptoms.

Some workplace environments carry significant cancer risks, particularly those in which employees are exposed to carcinogenic agents. These risks are concentrated in blue collar occupations, and are therefore potentially a greater factor for blacks and other minorities who, as a result of employment discrimination, are overrepresented in these occupations. An example would be those persons assigned to coke ovens in the steel industry, positions disproportionately held by blacks. The increase in cancer incidence and mortality among blacks in the 1950s and 1960s may be the result of the large rural to urban migration which brought blacks to the cities and towns which had these kind of industries.

Lead Poisoning

There is increasing realization that lead poisoning may be the most serious health problem facing black Americans. A decade ago it was a disease, often presented as encephalopathy, that was associated with the ingestion of lead paint. Now lead poisoning has been recognized as a largely "asymptomatic" condition, characterized by an elevated blood lead level, linked with many sources of exposure and affecting a broader range of children.

The most important lead hazards are leaded paint, dust, and soil. Until the 1950s paint contained as much as 50%, sometimes more, lead by dry weight. Direct ingestion of lead paint–the most concentrated source of lead–is most often the cause of high risk symptomatic or asymptomatic lead poisoning. However, dust and soil are also major sources. The effects of lead in dust and dirt are increased by small particle size, which enhances absorption, and by its continuing presence in children's environments. In particular, hand-to-mouth transfer of lead-contaminated dust and dirt enter a child's system through normal play. This often produces subclinical chronic lead intoxication, which constitutes over 90% of all childhood lead poisoning cases.

The most severe effects of lead (acute encephalopathy, seizures, coma, and death) occur at blood lead levels of 80 to 100 ug/dl and over. However, moderately elevated blood lead levels (as low as 25 ug/dl) have effects on central nervous system functions such as intelligence, behavior control, and fine motor coordination; they can produce neurological dysfunction and motor impairment. Further, metabolic effects occur in children with blood lead concentration as low as 10-15 ug/dl. Recent studies strongly suggest that even at subclinical levels of lead intoxication children sustain *permanent* cognitive and behavioral damage, manifested in poor school performance and a variety of learning disabilities.

Boston provides an example of how blacks are disproportionately affected by lead poisoning. Lead poisoning, while occurring throughout this city, is to a surprising degree concentrated within very limited geographic areas. Four neighborhoods–Dorchester, Roxbury, Jamaica Plain, and Mattapan–account for the highest numbers and percentages of children poisoned. These neighborhoods, containing 56% of the at-risk population (nine months to six years of age), account for 87% of the city's lead-poisoned children. Further, 16 of the census tracts in these neighborhoods–

containing less than 18% of the city's at-risk children–account for 41% of Boston's lead-poisoned children. These neighborhoods contain a major portion of the black population of Boston. Although blacks make up only 20% of the population of Boston, they are 78% of Roxbury, 81% of Mattapan, and over 20% of Dorchester.

AIDS

Acquired immune deficiency syndrome (AIDS) is increasingly becoming a disease of poor, African-American heterosexuals and their children who are residents of the inner-city. Though in general, homosexual/bisexual males remain the population at greatest risk, accounting for approximately two-thirds of the cumulative national cases, 39% of black males report exposure to the disease through homosexual/bisexual risk behaviors and 35% through intravenous (IV) drug use.

Precise figures of the incidence and prevalence of AIDS cases are poorly known, difficult to ascertain, and likely underestimate the true scope of the disease. However, as of June 1989, Centers for Disease Control data show a total number of 99,936 reported AIDS cases in the United States. The occurrence of these cases is disproportionately overrepresented in the black population. For example, although blacks compose only 12% of the U.S. population, they account for 26% of known AIDS cases. Among all risk groups, blacks are more likely than whites to get AIDS and, after diagnosis, have a shorter mean survival time than whites–8 months and 18 to 24 months respectively. Among all males in the U.S. with AIDS, 24% are black, and black males are 2.5 times as likely to get AIDS as white males; among all women with the disease, 54% are black, and black females are 12 times as likely as white females to contract the disease; among children with AIDS, 55% are black, and they are 15 times more likely to be afflicted than white children; and among IV drug users, the population where the virus is spreading fastest, four out of five afflicted with AIDS are black. IV drug use accounts for one-fourth of all new cases of AIDS, and it is not only drug users themselves who are at high risk, but their sex partners as well. Female sex partners, both drug users and nondrug users, can, as a result of perinatal transmission, infect a fetus in the womb or a newborn at birth. Indeed, over 75% of pediatric AIDS cases result from perinatal transmission; and of children who become infected perinatally, 75% have mothers who are either IV drug users or who are the sex partners of IV drug users.

It is an alarming fact that AIDS has become a leading cause of infant and child mortality, ranking ninth among children ages 1 to 4 years old, and seventh in young people ages 15 to 24 years old. It is projected that, if current trends continue, in the next three or four years, AIDS will be among the five leading causes of death in children. Though black children constitute only 15% of the nation's children, of the 1,681 cases of AIDS among children under age 13 years, over half of them are black. It is projected that by 1991, one out of ten U.S. pediatric hospital beds may be occupied by an AIDS patients.

Homicide

Total and age-adjusted homicide rates for the United States showed a relatively low base line in the 1950s, a sharp increase between 1960 and 1970, a continued rise during 1970, and a slight decrease beginning in the early 1980s. Among the most consistent findings is that blacks and men are more likely to be victims of homicide than whites and women. The highest rates of homicide mortality occurred among young black males, whereas the lowest rates occurred among elderly females. The frequency of homicide in a given population furnishes an index of reactions to the cumulative stresses in the group. Problems generated by these tragic losses are larger than a simple summation of individual misery. Ultimately, a high rate of homicide disrupts almost every facet of society. The magnitude of the homicide problem demands that coordinated actions be taken by the health sector and criminal justice system.

Access to Health Care

Although the introduction of Medicare and Medicaid in 1965 increased access to and availability of health care services for people over 65 and for many of the poor, these programs are now in jeopardy because of their association with significant increases in expenditures for health care. Twenty-five years later we are now witnessing uncertainties in health care financing that promise to widen the gap between those served adequately and those served inadequately by the health care system.

Unmet Health Care Needs

The combination of poverty, low levels of education, unemployment, and substandard housing has created a permanently underserved population within black communities in the nation. These interrelated factors are all associated with poor health status, as reflected by high rates of infant mortality. A greater prevalence of disease, in association with other indices of social disorganization that exist in these underserved communities, leaves this population particularly dependent upon health financing arrangements. Measures to remove health status deficits are costly.

Between 1980 and 1982 the number of people below 150% of the poverty level increased by 13.5%. During the same period the number of people with no health insurance or private, nongroup insurance increased by 7%. Although Medicaid coverage remained constant, the proportion of low income people covered fell from 36% to 31%. Additionally, the number of people who were both poor and inadequately insured increased by 20.9%. These trends strongly suggest an increasing need for imbursed care. However, during the same period, the volume of free care incr only 3.8%. Most private hospitals provided relatively little free care despite re ly strong financial pictures. Public hospitals in metropolitan areas did expan efforts in providing free care, but the limited availability of resources constrained the degree of expansion. In nonmetropolitan and rural areas the amount of free care provided by both public and private hospitals actually decreased during the two-year period.

Increased poverty, inadequate insurance, a relatively small increase in free care provided by hospitals, all had particularly serious consequence in black communities. Black Americans have been disproportionately represented among the poor, the unemployed, and the uninsured. In 1981, 32.2% of the black population was living in poverty, compared with 11.1% of the white population. In 1983 the unemployment rate of black Americans was 20.6% compared with 8.6% of white Americans. In 1980 86% of white Americans had private insurance; only 61% of black Americans had private insurance. Twenty percent of black Americans in the below-65 age group were insured by Medicaid, and 17.8% had no health insurance. Current trends which limit public funding disproportionately affect black Americans.

Use of Services Relative to Need

Although gross utilization of medical services by blacks sometimes exceeds that of whites, blacks still do not have equity of access. Equity of access is best considered in the context of whether people actually *in need* of medical care receive it. Blacks are in poorer health than whites, and consequently would be expected to have more physician visits. However, when utilization is compared to *need*, blacks obtain needed care less readily than whites.

When blacks do utilize available services, their care tends to be episodic, to lack continuity. While overall utilization statistics reveal few racial disparities, there are marked differences in the location, source, and quality of care for black health careseekers. Recent data indicate an average annual rate of office visits to physicians for coronary heart disease by nonwhites that is half that for whites—42 per 1,000 compared to 80 per 1,000. Office visits of all kinds by black patients tended to be to general and family practitioners (46.6%); 10.7% of visits were to internists, and 0.8% to cardiovascular disease (CVD) specialists. Black patients are much less likely than white patients to see CVD specialists. Visits to physicians in hospital clinics and emergency rooms constitute 11.2% of physician visits by whites and 25.6% of physician visits by blacks. In contrast, 69% of all visits by whites were to physicians' offices, compared with 58% of visits by blacks (13% versus 5%). Nonwhites (68%) are less likely to have a regular family doctor for their health care than are whites (78%).

Blacks and other minorities are overrepresented among families who report a need for medical care but fail to obtain it or are refused for financial reasons. Members of minority groups admitted to public-hospital emergency rooms for evaluation are sometimes transferred to other facilities, despite the risk of life-threatening arrhythmias, because of their inability to pay for medical care. "Patient dumping" for economic reasons appears widespread, and it disproportionally affects blacks. With the increased corporatization of medical care and the emerging dominance of for-profit health care, these trends, already disproportionately affecting blacks, are likely to worsen.

Not only does race affect *whether, when, how often, and where* medical care occurs, it also profoundly influences *what* services are received – assuming that contact with the system is made at all. For example, NCHS data indicate that the rate of cardiac catheterization among blacks (1.15 per 1,000 population) was only 60% of that reported for whites (1.93 per 1,000). Blacks diagnosed with coronary heart disease are less likely to undergo ECG than other races (2.7% to 3.3%). In 1982, only 4,000 out of 170,000 coronary bypass procedures were performed on black patients.

Black Health Professionals

The availability of health services is positively correlated with the supply of health professionals. While the Graduate Medical Education National Advisory Committee (GMENAC) projected a surplus of physicians by 1990, the supply of black physicians, dentists, and pharmacists will be inadequate. In 1980 there was one black physician (M.D. or D.O.) for every 2,264 black persons in the population, compared with one physician for every 647 persons in the general population. The disparity in these ratios for dentistry and pharmacy is even more striking, with one black dentist for every 7,297 black persons in the population and one black pharmacist for every 7,838 black persons, as compared with ratios for the general population of 1/1,795 and 1/1,571 for dentistry and pharmacy respectively. Because 87% of black physicians serve black patients, and 90.4% of nonblack physicians serve the white population, the disparity in ratios reflects a disparity in the availability of services.

Conclusion

Access to care is essential for treatment of the health problems discussed above. Yet black Americans make fewer office visits to physicians than whites and are less likely to be seen by specialists. Blacks have more difficulty in entering the medical care system than whites and express greater dissatisfaction with the services they receive.

The evidence concerning the rates of survival for cancer patients by stage of diagnosis suggests very strongly the need for early detection and early treatment. One avenue of early detection of a disease is periodic preventive checkups. But as we have seen, seeking medical care is a function of socioeconomic status. With disproportionately lower education and income blacks are less likely to have asymptomatic checkups.

The explanation that low income, less educated people use preventive services less and are less knowledgeable about appropriate health behavior because their culture does not place a high value on health is the "culture of poverty" view. This culture is seen as being passed from generation to generation, creating a cycle of poverty and poor health. Thus, the victim—the poor person in need of adequate services—is blamed for not acquiring such services.

An alternative perspective is the "structural" view, which assigns primary responsibility for the alienation of low income patients to their material disadvantage and to the systems barriers they face when seeking care. It suggests the need for changes in the training of health professionals and in the organization of care. It makes the assumption that "good" experiences will result in behavior change; if the client has positive experiences, more appropriate care-seeking behaviors will result.

This structural approach, which addresses the problem of negative individual experiences with medical care, should be joined by an approach that addresses the issue of equity of access to care. Many public health analysts have called for well-specified, targeted initiatives to address "pockets of inequity." However, broader based efforts must also be attempted. For example, there have been calls for increased emphasis on state-level approaches to solving health policy problems, including the establishment of programs to finance health services for "near poor" individuals who are unable to qualify for Medicaid. Proposals include providing direct insurance to individuals as well as financial support to local hospitals. One hopes that such efforts as these do not detract from the effort to develop a national health plan that is more comprehensive than the current provisions of Medicare and Medicaid.

Appendix

Assessment of the Status of African-Americans
Project Study Group Members

Project Leaders

Director: Wornie L. Reed, William Monroe Trotter Institute, University of
   Massachusetts at Boston

Co-Chair: James E. Blackwell, Department of Sociology, University of
   Massachusetts at Boston

Co-Chair: Lucius J. Barker, Department of Political Science, Washington University

Study Group on Education

Charles V. Willie (Chair), School of Education, Harvard University
Antoine M. Garibaldi (Vice-Chair), Department of Education, Xavier University
Robert A. Dentler, Department of Sociology, University of Massachusetts at Boston
Robert C. Johnson, Minority Studies Academic Program, St. Cloud State University
Meyer Weinberg, Department of Education, University of Massachusetts at Amherst

Study Group on Employment, Income, and Occupations

William Darity, Jr., (Chair) Department of Economics, University of North Carolina
Barbara Jones (Vice-Chair), College of Business, Prairies View A&M University
Jeremiah P. Cotton, Department of Economics, University of Massachusetts at
   Boston
Herbert Hill, Industrial Relations Research Institute, University of Wisconsin

Study Group on Political Participation
and the Administration of Justice

Michael B. Preston (Chair), Department of Political Science, University of Southern
   California
Diane M. Pinderhughes (Vice-Chair), Department of Political Science, University of
   Illinois/Champaign
Tobe Johnson, Department of Political Science, Morehouse College

Nolan Jones, Staff Director, Committee on Criminal Justice and Public Protection, National Governors Association

Susan Welch, Department of Political Science, University of Nebraska

John Zipp, Department of Sociology, University of Wisconsin-Milwaukee

Study Group on Social and Cultural Change

Alphonso Pinkney (Chair), Department of Sociology, Hunter College

James Turner (Vice-Chair), Africana Studies and Research Center, Cornell University

John Henrik Clarke, Department of Black and Puerto Rican Studies, Hunter College

Sidney Wilhelm, Department of Sociology, State University of New York-Buffalo

Study Group on Health Status and Medical Care

William Darity, Sr. (Chair), School of Public Health, University of Massachusetts at Amherst

Stanford Roman (Vice-Chair), Morehouse School of Medicine, Atlanta

Claudia Baquet, National Cancer Institute, Bethesda, Maryland

Noma L. Roberson, Department of Cancer Control and Epidemiology, Rockwell Park Institute

Study Group on the Family

Robert B. Hill (Chair), Morgan State University, Baltimore, Maryland

Andrew Billingsley (Vice-Chair), Department of Family and Community Development, University of Maryland

Eleanor Engram, Engram-Miller Associates, Cleveland, Ohio

Michelene R. Malson, School of Social Work, University of North Carolina

Roger H. Rubin, Department of Family and Community Development, University of Maryland

Carol B. Stack, Graduate School of Education, University of California-Berkeley

James B. Stewart, Black Studies Program, Pennsylvania State University

James E. Teele, Department of Sociology, Boston University

Contributors

Carolyne W. Arnold, College of Public and Community Services, University of
    Massachusetts at Boston
James Banks, School of Education, University of Washington
Margaret Beale Spencer, College of Education, Emory University
Bob Blauner, Department of Sociology, University of California, Berkeley
Larry Carter, Department of Sociology, University of Oregon
Obie Clayton, School of Criminal Justice, University of Nebraska
James P. Comer, Department of Psychiatry, Yale Medical School
Charles Flowers, Department of Education, Fisk University
Bennett Harrison, Urban and Public Affairs, Carnegie Mellon University
Norris M. Haynes, Child Study Center, New Haven
Joseph Himes, Department of Sociology, University of North Carolina at Greensboro
Hubert E. Jones, School of Social Work, Boston University
James M. Jones, Department of Psychology, University of Delaware
Faustine C. Jones-Wilson, *Journal of Negro Education*, Howard University
Barry A. Kreisberg, National Council on Crime and Delinquency, San Francisco
Hubert G. Locke, Society of Justice Program, University of Washington
E. Yvonne Moss, William Monroe Trotter Institute, University of Massachusetts at
    Boston
Willie Pearson, Jr., Department of Sociology, Grambling State University
Michael L. Radelet, Department of Sociology, University of Florida
Robert Rothman, *Education Week*, Washington, DC
Diana T. Slaughter, School of Education, Northwestern University
A. Wade Smith, Department of Sociology, Arizona State University
Leonard Stevens, Compact for Educational Opportunity, Milwaukee
Wilbur Watson, Department of Sociology, Atlanta University
Warren Whatley, Department of Economics, University of Michigan
John B. Williams, Affirmative Action Office, Harvard University
Rhonda Williams, Department of Economics, University of Maryland
Reginald Wilson, American Council of Education, Washington, DC